Foreign Policy Analysis

This exciting new book aims to reinvigorate the conversation between foreign policy analysis and international relations. It opens up the discussion, situating existing debates in foreign policy in relation to contemporary concerns in international relations, and provides a concise and accessible account of key areas in foreign policy analysis that are often ignored.

Focusing on how the process of foreign policy decision making affects the conduct of states in the international system, and analysing the relationship between policy, agency and actors, the work examines:

- Foreign policy decision making
- Foreign policy and bureaucracies
- Domestic sources of foreign policy
- Foreign policy and the state
- Foreign policy and globalization
- Foreign policy and change

This work builds on and expands the theoretical canvas of foreign policy analysis, shaping its ongoing dialogue with international relations and offering an important introduction to the field. It is essential reading for all students of foreign policy and international relations.

Chris Alden is a Reader in International Relations at the London School of Economics and Political Science.

Amnon Aran is a Lecturer in the Department of International Politics at City University London.

Foreign Policy Analysis

New approaches

Chris Alden and Amnon Aran

Routledge
Taylor & Francis Group

LONDON AND NEW YORK

First published 2012
by Routledge
2 Park Square, Milton Park, Abingdon, Oxon OX14 4RN

Simultaneously published in the USA and Canada
by Routledge
711 Third Avenue, New York, NY 10017

*Routledge is an imprint of the Taylor & Francis Group,
an informa business*

British Library Cataloguing in Publication Data
A catalogue record for this book is available from the British Library

Library of Congress Cataloging in Publication Data
Alden, Chris.
Foreign policy analysis : new approaches / Chris Alden and
Amnon Aran.
    p. cm.
Includes bibliographical references and index.
1. International relations. I. Aran, Amnon. II. Title.
JZ1242.A45 2011
327.1 – dc22   2011016295

ISBN: 978-0-415-42798-2 (hbk)
ISBN: 978-0-415-42799-9 (pbk)
ISBN: 978-0-203-64099-9 (ebk)

Typeset in Times
by Cenveo publisher services

Contents

Acknowledgements

We would like to thank the following people for their support and assistance with this book. To Craig Fowlie and Nicola Parkin of Routledge who provided us with the necessary time to complete this project. Cynthia Little has done a wonderful job of copy editing our book, Professors Margot Light and Christopher Hill, and the late Professor Fred Halliday, who provided inspiration for this book at different times and in different ways, deserve our sincere gratitude. Professor Kim Hutchings of the Department of International Relations at LSE and Professor Maxi Schoeman of the Department of Political Sciences, University of Pretoria, supported Chris Alden's sabbatical and made the completion of the manuscript possible. To Filippo Dionigi for being an excellent research assistant.

Finally our respective families – Kato, Rachel. Jonathan and Amelia, Shani, Yoav and Assaf – for all their love, care and support.

Acronyms

ANC	African National Congress
BBC	British Broadcasting Corporation
BPM	bureaucratic politics model
CW	Cold War
DFA	Department of Foreign Affairs
EU	European Union
FPA	foreign policy analysis
GT	globalization theory
HS	historical sociology
IEMP	ideology, economic, military, political
IMF	International Monetary Fund
IR	international relations
MNC	multinational corporation
NATO	North Atlantic Treaty Organization
NGO	non-governmental organization
SOP	standard operating procedure
TNA	transnational actor
UK	United Kingdom
UN	United Nations
US	United States
WHS	Weberian historical sociology
WWII	World War II

1 Foreign policy analysis – an overview

Introduction

Foreign policy analysis (FPA) is the study of the conduct and practice of relations between different actors, primarily states, in the international system. Diplomacy, intelligence, trade negotiations and cultural exchanges all form part of the substance of foreign policy between international actors. At the heart of the field is an investigation into decision making, the individual decision makers, processes and conditions that affect foreign policy and the outcomes of these decisions. By adopting this approach, FPA is necessarily concerned not only with the actors involved in the state's formal decision-making apparatus, but also with the variety of sub-national sources of influence upon state foreign policy. Moreover, in seeking to provide a fuller explanation for foreign policy choice, scholars have had to take account of the boundaries between the state's internal or domestic environment and the external environment.

FPA developed as a separate area of enquiry within the discipline of international relations (IR), due both to its initially exclusive focus on the actual conduct of inter-state relations and to its normative impulse. While IR scholars understood their role as being to interpret the broad features of the international system, FPA specialists saw their mandate as being a concentration on actual state conduct and the sources of decisions. The FPA focus on the foreign policy process as opposed to foreign policy outcomes, is predicated on the belief that closer scrutiny of the actors, their motivations, the structures of decision making and the broader context within which foreign policy choices are formulated would provide greater analytical purchase. Moreover, scholars working within FPA saw their task as normative, that is to say, as aimed at improving foreign policy decision making to enable states to achieve better outcomes and, in some instances, even to enhance the possibility of peaceful relations between states.

In the context of David Singer's well-known schema of IR, in grappling with world politics, one necessarily focuses on studying the phenomena at the international system level, the state (or national) level, or the individual level.[1] FPA has traditionally emphasized the state and individual levels as the key areas for understanding the nature of the international system. At the same time, as the rise in the number and density of transnational actors (TNAs) has transformed the international system, making interconnectivity outside of traditional state-to-state conduct more likely, FPA has had to expand its own outlook to account for an increasingly diverse range of non-state actors, such as global environmental activists or multinational corporations (MNCs).

An underlying theme within the study of FPA is the 'structure-agency' debate.[2] As in other branches of the social sciences, FPA scholars are divided as to the degree of influence to accord to structural factors (the constraints imposed by the international system) and human agency (the role of individual choice in shaping the international system) when analysing foreign policy decisions and decision-making environments. However, the FPA focus on the process of foreign policy formulation, the role of decision makers and the nature of foreign policy choice has tended to produce a stronger emphasis on agency than is found in IR (at least until the advent of the 'constructivism turn' in the 1990s). Thus, early analyses of foreign policy decision making recognized from the outset the centrality of subjective factors in shaping and interpreting events, actors and foreign policy choices. Writing in 1962, Richard Snyder and colleagues pointed out that 'information is selectively perceived and evaluated in terms of the decision maker's frame of reference. Choices are made in the basis of preferences which are in part situationally and in part biographically determined.'[3] Indeed, as the chapters in this book show, in many respects, FPA anticipates key insights and concerns associated with the reflexivist or constructivist tradition.[4]

FPA has much in common with other policy-oriented fields that seek to employ scientific means to understand phenomena. Debate within FPA over the utility of different methodological approaches, including rational choice, human psychology and organizational studies, has encouraged the development of a diversity of material and outlooks on foreign policy. This apparently eclectic borrowing from other fields, at least as seen by other IR scholars, in fact reflects this intellectual proximity to the changing currents of thinking within the various domains of the policy sciences.[5] At the same time, there remains a significant strand of FPA which, like diplomatic studies, owes a great debt to historical method. Accounting for the role of history in shaping foreign policy – be it the identity of a particular nation-state, conflicting definitions of a specific foreign policy issue or their use (and misuse) as analogous in foreign policy decision making – is a rich area of study in FPA.

Set within this context our book aims to revisit the key question motivating foreign policy analysts, that is, how the process of foreign policy decision making affects the conduct of states in the international system and the relationship between agency, actors and foreign policy, which is crucial for a reinvigoration of the conversation between FPA and IR. Our book seeks to open up this discussion by situating existing debates in FPA in relation to contemporary concerns in IR and providing an account of areas that for the most part in FPA have been studiously ignored. What follows is a brief summary of some of the key theoretical approaches and innovations that have featured in FPA as scholars have attempted to address the questions of who makes foreign policy, how is it made and what influences the process. We refer to this body of literature as Classical FPA. We explore the main features of Classical FPA and identify three areas that have been overlooked by scholars. For instance, in FPA there is no *theory of the state*, no meaningful incorporation of the systemic changes provoked by *globalization* and no comprehensive accounting for *change* in foreign policy. This is followed by a brief elaboration on these shortcomings through our presentation of three critiques of FPA.

Realism: the state, national interest and foreign policy

The roots of FPA lie in its reaction to the dominance of realism and its depiction of the state and its interactions with other states, whether through direct bilateral relations or through multilateral institutions such as the United Nations (UN), and a general dissatisfaction with realism's ability to provide credible explanations of foreign policy outcomes. In keeping with the realist paradigm, the state is seen as a unitary and rational actor, rendering it unnecessary to analyse the role of the discrete components of government (either the executive or the legislature) in order to assess state foreign policy. In this context, a key concept in the traditional realist canon is 'national interest'. Although a much-disputed term, national interest remains a central preoccupation of foreign policy decision makers and a reference point for realist scholars seeking to interpret state action. Hans Morgenthau defines national interest as synonymous with power and, therefore, both the proper object of a state's foreign policy and the best measure of its capacity to achieve its aims.[6]

What constitutes national interest, how it is determined and ultimately implemented are crucial to understanding the choices and responses pursued by states in international affairs. Realists assert that the character of the international system, that is, its fundamentally anarchic nature, is the most important guide to interpreting foreign policy. The pursuit of security and the efforts to enhance material wealth place states in competition with other states, limiting the scope for cooperation to a series of selective, self-interested strategies. In this setting, the centrality of power – especially manifested as military power – is seen to be the key determinant of a state's ability to sustain a successful foreign policy. Geographic position, material resources and demography are other important components of this equation.

Realists believe that all states' foreign policies conform to these basic parameters and that scholars above all need to investigate the influences of the structure of the international system and the relative power of states in order to understand the outcomes of foreign policy decisions. Calculation of national interest is self-evident; it can be arrived at rationally through careful analysis of the material conditions of states as well as the particulars of a given foreign policy dilemma confronting states.

Scholars such as Richard Snyder and his colleagues, frustrated by the facile rendering of international events in established IR circles, issued a call to move beyond this systemic orientation and 'open the black box' of foreign policy decision making. Rather than producing a normative critique of realism (something that later would become commonplace in academia), Snyder, Rosenau and others were intent primarily on finding an improved methodological approach to assessing interactions between states.[7] And, while in creating the field of FPA these scholars accepted key tenets of realism such as the centrality of the state in IR, they also set in motion a series of investigative strands that ultimately would contribute to an expansion of the knowledge and understanding about the relationship between foreign policy and IR.

Behaviourism and rationalism

The original studies by FPA scholars in the 1950s and 1960s posed some explicit challenges to the realist assumptions in ascendancy in the field of IR at that time. Instead of examining the *outcomes* of foreign policy decisions, behaviourists sought to understand the *process* of foreign policy decision making. In particular, scholars such as Robert Jervis, Harold Sprout and Margaret Sprout investigated the role of the individual decision maker and the accompanying influences on foreign policy choice. They believed that shining a spotlight on the decision maker would allow them to unpack the key variables linked directly to studies of human agency which contribute to foreign policy decision making.

This 'behaviourist' approach with its focus on the 'minds of men' came at a time when those working on decision making in the policy sciences were increasingly enamoured with the notion of applying a set of fixed rules to understand the process and outcomes of decision making. The methodology, which came to be known as rational choice theory, amongst other things posited a unified decision-making body in the form of the state, as well as a belief that the pursuit of self-interest guided all decision makers. Since rational choice strongly adhered to some of the key ideas of realism, it was relatively easy for rationalism and realism to find common cause in their assessment of the world of international politics.

The emphasis on individual decision makers in FPA led scholars to focus on psychological and cognitive factors as explanatory sources of foreign policy choice. For instance, Jervis asserts that the psychological disposition of a leader, the cognitive limits imposed by the sheer volume of information available to decision makers and the inclination to opt for what are clearly second-best policy options, all contribute to imperfect foreign policy outcomes. For Kenneth Boulding, it is the set of beliefs, biases and stereotypes, which he characterizes as the 'image' held by decision makers, that play the most important role in shaping foreign policy decisions. In addition, other scholars point out that the decision-making process itself is subject to the vagaries of group dynamics while the constraints imposed by crises introduce further distortions to foreign policy choice.[8]

The result was a comprehensive critique by FPA scholars of many of the key findings related to foreign policy in the realist and emerging rationalist perspectives. At the same time, while the policy sciences continued to move towards elaborating rational choice theory, those FPA scholars working in the rationalist tradition sought to find a way to reconcile their insights into the effects of psychology and cognition on foreign policy decision making, with some account of rational decision making. This effort characterises foreign policy making as a far less organized, consistent and rational process than depicted by the realists. Psychology constrains rationality; human divisions and disagreements challenge the notion that the state is a unitary actor.

Equally significant was the introduction of what could be called a 'proto-constructivist' strand within FPA, which asserted the subjectivity of the decision maker and, concurrently, the notion that foreign policy was the product of mutually constitutive processes that involved individuals, societies and the construction of an 'other'. Chapter 2 explores this literature more fully.

Bureaucratic politics and foreign policy

The focus on the individual decision maker, despite the insights it produced, was seen by some FPA scholars to be excessively narrow. Even within states, the conflicting outlooks and demands of foreign policy bureaucracies, such as the ministries of trade and of defence, clearly influence foreign policy decisions in ways that reflect the primacy of parochial concerns over considerations of national interest. While the executive decision maker was clearly a key component of the foreign policy decision-making process, it had to be recognized that any decisions made took place within the context of institutions specifically charged with interpreting and implementing foreign and security policy for the state. The role and contribution of specialized ministries, departments and agencies – supplemented by ad hoc working groups tasked with a particular foreign policy mandate – needed to be accounted for in FPA.

Drawing on organizational theory and sociology, scholars sought to capture the manner in which institutional motivations and procedures impacted upon the foreign policy process. For Graham Allison, Morton Halperin and others, an analysis of foreign policy decision making had to start with these bureaucracies and the various factors that caused them to play what, in their view, was the determining role in shaping foreign policy outcomes. Their approach emphasized the interplay between leaders, bureaucratic actors, organizational culture and, to an extent, political factors outside the formal apparatus of the state.[9]

Broader in reach than the behaviourists' single focus on the individual decision maker, advocates of the bureaucratic politics approach to FPA began a process of investigation into sources of influence over foreign policy that went beyond the actors directly involved in the formal decision-making apparatus. This search opened the way for consideration of the role of societal factors, such as interest groups, in influencing public opinion, all of which ultimately contributed to a radical rethinking of the importance of the state itself in IR. Chapter 3 provides a more complete overview of this literature.

Domestic structures and foreign policy

In moving away from a focus on the individual decision maker and the state bureaucracy, FPA scholars began to show an interest in the domestic, societal sources of foreign policy. This interest produced a rich literature which we describe as the domestic structure approach. One of its strands deals with the effects of the material attributes of a country, such as size, location, agricultural and industrial potential, demographic projections, etc., on foreign policy.[10] A second category develops a more sophisticated notion of the domestic structure. Thomas Risse-Kappen and Haral Muller's work, for instance, deals 'with the nature of the political institutions (the state), with the basic features of the society, and with the institutional and organisational arrangements linking state and society and channelling societal demands into the political system'.[11] The debate on the emergence of democratic peace theory is an interesting illustration of how FPA used the domestic structure approach to explain foreign policy. Advocates of democratic peace theory argue that democracies inherently produce a more peaceful foreign policy, at least as far as relations with other democratic states are concerned. An intriguing debate followed this assertion, probing the degree to which the nature of the polity can account for the conduct of foreign policy.[12] Chapter 4 explores this literature.

Pluralism: linkage politics and foreign policy

While the previous three approaches sought to understand FPA through recourse to the structure of the international system, the decision-making process within states and the societal sources of foreign policy, there is a fourth, pluralist, interpretation of foreign policy. Pluralists do not believe that states are the only significant actors in international politics. They maintain that, at least from the 1970s (but perhaps even earlier), the increased linkages between a variety of state, sub-state and non-state actors have eroded the traditional primacy of the state in foreign policy. Indeed, one of the central features of the globalizing world is the possibility that MNCs could exercise de facto foreign policy based on their financial resources, or that non-governmental organizations (NGOs) wield power through their ability to mobilize votes. For pluralists, crucial for an understanding of foreign policy outcomes is analysis of the influences derived from domestic and transnational sources – not necessarily tied to the state. The pluralist approach portrays the transnational environment as an unstructured, mixed actor environment. It is unstructured in so far as it is 'entirely actor generated' and 'it is difficult to distinguish the intentional from the incidental'.[13] It is a mixed actor environment to the extent that state and non-state actors either coexist or compete. This pluralist environment of complex interdependency effectively diminishes the scope of state action in foreign policy making, to that of management of a diversity of forces within the domestic sphere including government, and outside the boundaries of the state.[14]

Robert Putnam's 'two-level game' attempts to capture the challenges imposed by complex interdependency on foreign policy decision makers. Writing in the rationalist tradition, he suggests that the decision-making process involves both a domestic arena where one set of rules and interests governs, and an international arena, where a different set of rules and interests prevail. Balancing the logic and demands of the two arenas, which often are in conflict, forms the central dilemma of foreign policy making as seen by pluralists.[15] Other scholars, such as Joe Hagan, incorporate particular features of the domestic structure in the form of regimes and autonomous political actors (e.g. factions, parties, institutions) into the decision-making rubric.[16] The pluralist literature captures well the trends that have shaped the external environment in which foreign policy operates. It also examines many of the issues in the vast literature on globalization. For example, scholars such as Hill argue that the pluralist literature is better equipped than the literature on globalization to explore the implications of issues of concern to each for foreign policy. We explore this proposition in Chapter 6, which examines the relationship between foreign policy and globalization and the implications it might have for the study of FPA.

Three critiques of 'Classical' FPA: bringing in the state, globalization and change

This brief overview of the field of FPA shows that there are many different ways of understanding the conduct and significance of states and sub-state and non-state actors in foreign policy making. Though there is no consensus amongst these approaches, each is seen to contribute to a fuller picture of how states and, ultimately, the international system, work. Indeed, FPA illumines much that is obscure in IR (a shortcoming somewhat grudgingly acknowledged by recent developments such as neo-classical realism). While IR emphasizes the role and influence of structural constraints on the international system, FPA focuses on the inherent possibilities of human agency and sub-national actors to affect and even change the international system.

These features of Classical FPA have preoccupied foreign policy analysts for decades, providing a foundation for a steady accretion of knowledge, primarily through an elaboration of the established literature and detailed case studies, all of which is contributing to a maturing research agenda. At the same time, we would contend that there are oversights and areas that are neglected in Classical FPA, which is hampering development of the field. As already mentioned, these include the fact that there is no theory of the state in FPA, no meaningful incorporation of the systemic changes brought by globalization and no accounting for change in foreign policy.

FPA and the state

In highlighting the importance of such elements as human agency and sub-national actors, FPA has significantly enhanced our understanding of foreign policy making and its implementation. However, this analytical achievement comes at a conceptual price. In focusing on an unpacking of the realist black box, FPA failed to develop its own conception of the state with the result that the state is reduced to nothing more than the various actors responsible for foreign policy making. For example, early studies focus on the individual and de facto equate the state with the decision makers, thus rendering the state as no more than the sum of its individual (human) parts. In the bureaucratic politics approach, the state is little more than an arena in which competing fiefdoms engage in their inward-looking games. The state is ultimately no more than the sum of its bureaucratic units. From this perspective, foreign policy is either formulated by chance, or is captured unpredictably by different bureaucratic elements at different times.[17]

The domestic structure approach would seem more useful for conceptualizing the state, however, it does not provide a conceptualization of what the state is. Rather, as the debate on democratic peace theory and foreign policy forcefully shows, the state is equated with the polity. Consequently, it is treated more as *an arena* (not an actor) in which the social and political values of a given polity are manifested in its foreign policy. Finally, in pluralist formulations and Putnam's two-level game the principal role of the state is to mediate between the pressures from the domestic and the external spheres. These pressures arise from the socio-political activity in the domestic and transnational spheres, the inter-state activity occurring within the international realm and the principal motivations of the central executive. Hence, in contrast to earlier approaches, the state is rooted *simultaneously* in the domestic and the external spheres. In this respect, the pluralist approach and Putnam's metaphor of a two-level game are more useful than methods that accommodate the activities of actors in *either* the domestic *or* the international sphere. However, capturing the dual anchoring of state in the domestic and external spheres does not amount to a conception of the state. In this formulation the state is no more than the sum of the pressures exerted by external and domestic forces, derived from the activities that occur across the domestic–statist–transnational axis. The lack of a conceptualization of the state in FPA's key middle-range theories produced conceptual, ontological and epistemological tensions within FPA. These tensions are explored and addressed in Chapter 5.

FPA and globalization

FPA's notion of the state (or lack thereof) is not the only conceptual task we tackle in this book. Since the 1980s, a stimulating and charged debate on globalization has been taking place in the social sciences, including IR. In their work, *Global Transformations* (1999), Held et al. bring together the vast literature on globalization, laying the foundations for Globalization Theory (GT) and provide the tools for examining empirically the globalization of multiple activities: from politics and organized violence, to finance, trade, production and migration, culture and environmental degradation.[18] Held et al.'s appraisal of the hyperglobalist, global-sceptic and transformationalist theses defined the contours of the first great debate on globalization, placing the transformationalist thesis at the forefront of what emerged as GT.[19] Two broad assumptions unite the huge literature comprising GT. First, that globalization is producing a fundamental shift in the spatio-temporal constitution of human societies. Second, that this shift is so profound that, in retrospect, it has revealed a basic lacuna in the classical, territorially grounded tradition of social theory, promoting the development of a new post-classical social theory in which the categories of space and time assume a central, explanatory role.[20]

Since publication of *Global Transformations,* another great debate on globalization has emerged, much of it centring on the direction that GT should take. Authors, such as Rosenberg, argue that GT is fundamentally flawed,[21] hence, the way forward is to perform a post-mortem, to expose its 'follies' and draw lessons from these follies. Others acknowledge that the debate on globalization has generated a useful and insightful body of literature, but are resistant to attempts to turn it into a 'theory'.[22] This reluctance to theorize, and Rosenberg's dismissal of GT, are rejected by Scholte, Albert, Robertson and by Held and colleagues' ongoing work. Nevertheless, all these authors concede that GT faces a real challenge: how to develop beyond the formulations generated by the first great debate on globalization.[23]

In similar vein, we try to address what would appear to be a significant lacuna in GT and FPA. An examination of some of the best-known works and forums on globalization reveals that foreign policy is virtually excluded from GT.[24] Similarly, scholars of FPA have excluded GT from their matrix. For instance, the studies by Smith et al. and Hudson on the state of the art in FPA completely ignore globalization and GT,[25] while Hill argues that existing transnational formulations in FPA are better equipped than GT to examine issues that are of common concern to these literatures.[26] Webber and Smith, on the other hand, embrace the notion of globalization and explore its implications for FPA, but do not consider the reverse position.[27]

This mutual exclusion in our view is somewhat problematic since the relationship between foreign policy and globalization might have significant implications for the subject matter of IR. Thus, the gap in contemporary IR theory, framed by the mutual conceptual neglect of FPA and GT, would seem significant. Chapter 6 explores ways to bridge this gap and how we might conceptualize foreign policy in the context of globalization, to try to establish how and to what extent FPA can contribute to the study of foreign policy in the context of globalization, and to understand the relationship between these two aspects.

FPA and change

Finally, alongside the failure adequately to theorize the state and to account for the forces of globalization, *foreign policy change* has been rather ignored by classical FPA scholars. Similar to IR, which failed to account for the rapid series of events that precipitated the ending of the Cold War (CW) in 1989, FPA says little about the sources and conditions giving rise to significant alterations in a state's foreign policy. This is despite seminal foreign policy moments, such as Nixon's dramatic diplomatic turn to the People's Republic of China in 1972, and the systematic reorientation of post-Soviet states towards the west, when foreign policy change was a significant feature of the fabric of international politics.

Understanding and integrating 'change' into analyses of foreign policy requires accounting for its impact in relation to individual decision makers, institutions and structures of decision making as well as the wider socio-political and external context within which such change occurs. David Welch's *Painful Choices: A Theory of Foreign Policy Change* (2005) is one of the few efforts to tackle this subject. Welch tries to capture some of the diverse sources of foreign policy change by focusing on cognitive and motivational psychology, insights from organizational theory and, most successfully, by employing prospect theory. In the latter, foreign policy change is linked to decision makers' fears that continuing with the status quo will generate ever more painful losses.[28]

However, there is clearly much more scope for assessing the role of change in foreign policy. Drawing on other relevant sources, the literature on 'learning' provides insights into the part played by personality in facilitating foreign policy choices that embrace change.[29] If we examine the topic from a different angle, institutional sources of *resistance to change* may be tied to the levels of bureaucratic embeddedness in the decision-making process through role socialization, procedural scripts and cultural rationales, but there is little discussion in FPA of processes such as institutional learning and its impact on foreign policy choice.[30] Michael Barnett's analysis of how skilful 'political entrepreneurs' are able to re-frame identity issues within a specific institutional context so as to embark on dramatic foreign policy shifts, provides a theoretically eclectic treatment of foreign policy change which reasserts the role of agency.[31] Finally, against the backdrop of a 'wave of democratization' that has been sweeping across all regions of the world since 1974, a fruitful avenue for assessing foreign policy change is the relationship between regime type and socio-political changes in conjunction with broader systemic factors. Alison Stanger, building on the work of transitologists, such as Juan Linz and Samuel Huntington, suggests that it is the nature of democratic transitions – whether elite-led reformist regimes, revolutionary regimes or power-sharing arrangements – that shape the underlying approach adopted by a post-authoritarian regime to foreign policy questions.[32] How FPA might more fully account for change is explored in Chapter 7.

Conclusion: FPA and the study of IR

FPA has constantly engaged with the broader debates in the discipline of IR, from challenges to realism's key concepts, to introducing IR to new literatures, to employing a new type of methodology – that of a middle-range theory. We believe that if FPA is to maintain its status as an innovative sub-strand of IR, it is essential that it engages with the discipline. As we develop our three critiques of FPA, we will highlight new points of intersection between FPA and IR theory. Two strands of IR appear particularly useful for the development of an ongoing dialogue between FPA and broader IR theory: historical sociology of international relations, and constructivism. Engaging more closely with the broader debate in the social sciences on globalization and its implications for IR would also seem pertinent. Finally, FPA has potential points of intersection with neo-classical realism, which we explore in later chapters. Through this effort, we hope to be able to build on and expand the theoretical canvas of FPA and to shape its ongoing dialogue with IR.

2   Foreign policy decision making

Introduction

The foreign policy decision-making process is a major focus of FPA scholarship seeking to unlock and explain the complexities of state conduct in the international system. In this regard, rationality and its application to foreign policy decision making is one of the most influential approaches to understanding contemporary international politics. Derived from public choice theory (which itself emerged out of the fields of economics and policy sciences), rational choice scholars have actively sought to utilize a well-established methodology of decision making to enhance and assess foreign policy decision making. Applying this approach to the task of modelling the complex environment of foreign policy decision making has, nonetheless, posed new challenges for rationalists.[1] The result has been the development of innovations in modelling choice in areas as diverse as nuclear strategy and trade negotiations, which have become influential in academic and foreign policy making circles.

The use of rationalist approaches to analyse foreign policy decision making, at the same time, has inspired considerable commentary and criticism. Indeed, the formative work of FPA has been devoted to assessing the weaknesses of this school of thought and its links to realist assumptions.[2] This critique of rationalist accounts of foreign policy decision making is rooted as much in its inability to accurately capture the actual foreign policy process as in the problems posed by some of its foundational assumptions. Culling from studies of political psychology and cognitive theory, FPA scholars have focused on the centrality of the mind of the decision maker, its powerful effect on the framing of particular foreign policy issues and the consequent impact on the formulation and selection of policy options. The subsequent research conducted into the role of perceptual factors and cognitive shortcomings highlights the many distortions integral to the decision-making process, challenging the very possibility of achieving rationality in foreign policy.

Yet there remains within much of FPA a desire to retain adherence to a broadly rationalist description of foreign policy decision making. Notions such as 'bounded rationality', which seek to account for the distorting effects of partial information and narrowing perceptions, are suggestive of the continuing relevance of rational choice theory – albeit somewhat reconstituted in light of criticisms – to any accounts of the decision-making process. James Rosenau's clarion call to identify variables and rigorous methodologies to better organize the study of foreign policy – which led to the ill-fated comparative foreign policy research programme – while embracing much of the critique of rationalism in setting out his FPA 'pre-theories' nonetheless seeks to frame the research agenda squarely within the realm of positivism.[3] The 'pull of rationalism' as a method, however attenuated to account for critiques, remains an important dimension of FPA. The result is that contemporary scholars have developed new methodological approaches to foreign policy decision making which are explicitly aimed at reconciling the contingencies of rationality with the insights derived from its various critics.

Rationality and foreign policy decision making

Realists believe that all states' foreign policies conform to basic parameters set by the anarchic international system and that above all scholars need to investigate the influences of the structure of the international system and the relative power of states in order to understand the outcomes of foreign policy decisions. Calculations of national interest are self-evident and can be arrived at rationally through a careful analysis of the material conditions of states as well as the particulars of a given foreign policy dilemma confronting states. The classical realism formulation of balance of power provides a crude, but effective, tool for analysing state action in international affairs.

Rational choice theory (sometimes called public choice theory) as applied to international affairs has sought to introduce a more rigorous, methodologically sound approach that could use the basic laws of choice to assess the process and outcome of foreign policy decision making. From this perspective, the maximization of utility by actors – in this case, states – is the ultimate aim of foreign policy decision makers. By maximization of utility, we mean that a state first identifies and prioritizes foreign policy goals; it then identifies and selects from the means available to it which fulfil its aims with the least cost. This cost-benefit analysis involves trade-offs between different possible foreign policy positions and, ultimately, produces a theory of foreign policy choice that reflects a calculus of self-interest. In this regard, the focus of this approach traditionally is on policy outcomes and therefore assumes a relatively undifferentiated decision-making body for foreign policy (a 'unitary actor') rather than one composed of different decision makers.

However, some rationalist scholars have recognized that an assessment of national interest – defined as enhancing security and wealth maximization (or, to use the public choice jargon, 'preference formation') – is crucial to determining the actual foreign policy choice. Their consideration of the sources for foreign policy preferences suggests that it is the nature of the international system and accompanying structural parity between states produced by sovereignty, rather than any particular domestic feature in a given state, that remains the most significant determinant of choice. As all states reside within the same international setting in which the conditions of anarchy tend to structure the 'rules of the game' in a similar fashion for all states, coming to an interpretation of action and reaction should not be out of reach for foreign policy analysts.

Operationalising the core assumptions in rational decision making, especially those of motivation (self-interest) and a single decision maker (unitary actor), can produce some compelling explanations of the process and choices pursued in foreign policy. This general depiction of rationality is best captured perhaps through the application of game theory to foreign policy decision making. Here scholars have isolated particular dilemmas in foreign policy and sought to frame them within a matrix of choice that illuminates the dilemmas facing decision makers.

Game theory is a structured approach which in its original form posits a relatively simple matrix of participants and issues that allows mathematically derived interpretations of decision making. For game theorists, the respective rules of different types of games frame the possibilities of choice undertaken by the participants and the accompanying strategies employed to achieve best possible outcomes. For instance, cooperative and non-cooperative forms of the game produce strategies that range from 'zero-sum' wins by one participant over the other to trade-offs that secure 'win-sets', that is outcomes in which both parties are able to claim satisfactory – if often sub-optimal – outcomes. Snyder and Diesing employ game theory to develop an understanding of the conduct of states during international crises, coming up with nine possible negotiating 'games' framed by different crisis situations: 'Hero', 'Leader', 'Prisoner's Dilemma', 'Chicken', 'Deadlock', 'Called Bluff', 'Bully', 'Big Bully' and 'Protector'.[4] The central contention in this approach is that it is the structure of the crisis that determines the type of bargaining strategies and eventual outcomes that take place between two parties. Powell shifts the focus to the nature of the negotiation itself during international crises, positing that there is a 'risk/return' trade-off operating during international crises that is tied to power as well as information asymmetries.[5] Drawing on 'game theory' approaches, three useful examples of this form of rationalism put to the task of understanding foreign policy decision making can be applied in the areas of nuclear strategy, international trade and democratic peace theory.

Thomas Schelling's work on game theory and its application to nuclear strategy elaborates upon the classic prisoner's dilemma schema. Schelling uses the format of strategic bargaining with imperfect information in a non-cooperative game to adduce the conduct of participants facing decisions in a nuclear arms race.[6] His insight is to analyse how deterrence, that is, the promulgation of an arms build-up and a concomitant agreement not to mobilize ('first strike' in nuclear parlance), operates as an imperfect restraint on a state's move towards conflict. The incremental use of strategies of escalation to produce behaviour change in an aggressive opponent, or 'brinkmanship', is advocated by Schelling as a way of establishing and maintaining the credibility of the deterrent. A 'balance of terror' is the predicted foreign policy outcome in this approach and, indeed, served as the core nuclear doctrine for the United States (US) for a number of years.

In the area of international diplomacy, Robert Putnam attempts to explain the contrary outcomes found in trade policy negotiations.[7] Putnam asserts that the best way to understand the behaviour of foreign policy decision makers is to recognize that they are in fact operating in two separate environments, each with a distinctive set of logics that structure choice accordingly. Leaders naturally attend to domestic concerns in developing their position on a given issue. The fact that the international environment is a 'self-help system' conditioned by anarchy while the domestic environment functions in accordance with a recognized authority structure and accompanying rules, means that foreign policy decision makers have to operate in two overlapping – and potentially conflicting – games simultaneously. For Putnam, a win-set is only achieved when the outcome reflects the shared interests of all the relevant actors and is in tune with the imperatives of the domestic environment.

Finally, Levy and Razin's study of democratic peace theory provides a compelling interpretation of the role that information plays in open societies, which allows for them to devise bargaining strategies that produce both cooperation and mutually beneficial outcomes. According to Levy and Razin, it is the flow of information – a by-product of democratic societies – that better enables democratic decision makers to calculate potential gains and losses and thereby to come to an amicable resolution to any dispute.[8] By contrast, it is the uncertainties founded in information asymmetries in the interactions between democratic and non-democratic states that are the determining factor in explaining the statistical tendency towards foreign policies of conflict between them.

What is notable about the utilization of game theory in foreign policy decision making is the degree to which it tacitly relies upon the *perceptions* of decision makers in structuring the context of negotiations and the process that accompanies them. The lack of explicit recognition by rational choice theorists of the implications that this crucial perceptual factor has on key claims of rationality of the entire process opens up a line of criticism which FPA scholars such as Robert Jervis were to pursue with great vigour.[9]

With respect to the last two applications of game theory to foreign policy, outlined above, it is interesting that they involve greater attention to and integration of the domestic environment and, consequently, a richer description of the decision-making process. At the same time, however, as inputs from the domestic environment are integrated into the decision matrix the complexity of sources of influence upon the foreign policy decision-making process is increasingly evident. Rationalists operating in this tradition acknowledge that domestic constraints and the disparity between the underlying governing logic of the international and domestic systems exert a determining impact upon foreign policy decisions.[10] This fundamental condition helps explain the variety of foreign policy choices and outcomes which, on the surface, appear at odds with rationalist depictions of foreign policy. Indeed, the putative pressure from domestic sources is even said to be exploited by leaders to extract concessions during negotiations with foreign actors.[11]

More generally, as can be seen from this presentation of the rationalist perspective on foreign policy – and notwithstanding the nagging problems associated with individual perceptions and the complexity implied by giving greater weight to domestic factors – developing foreign policy goals and implementing them involves a relatively straightforward assessment of the situation and other actors' potential actions based on their status and material endowment within the international system. Optimal outcomes, albeit within the framework of available choices, are both the goal and the guide for foreign policy choice. Good foreign policy is achievable and, presumably, is a realistic source for ordering the international system through some form of balancing or trade-off mechanism.

Challenging rational decision making: the role of psychology, cognition and personality

Foreign policy is the product of human agency, that is, individuals in leadership positions identifying foreign policy issues, making judgements about them and then acting upon that information. It is this fundamental insight, at the heart of the behaviourist critique of rationality in decision making, which instigated a concentrated study of the impact of individual psychology on foreign policy. Underlying this behaviourist approach was the recognition that individual leaders of states exercise a seminal influence over the foreign policy process by dint of their experience, outlook and limitations and, therefore, were worthy of special attention. Among the diversity of psychological factors said to play a role in shaping foreign policy are the influence of individual perceptions, human cognition, a leader's personality and the dynamics of group decision making.

For proponents of the psychological approach, foreign policy decision makers operate in a highly complex world and their decisions carry significant risks. These include linguistic-cultural barriers, stereotypes, high volumes of, yet incomplete, information. Hence, through processes of perception and cognition, decision makers develop images, subjective assessments of the larger operational context, which when taken together constitute a 'definition of the situation'. These definitions are always a distortion of reality since the purpose of perception is to simplify and order the external environment. Policy makers can therefore never be completely rational in applying the rationalists' imperative of maximization of utility towards any decisions.

A critique of rational decision making

Harold and Margaret Sprout introduced one of the most defining critiques of the rational approach to foreign policy. They examined the environment within which foreign policy decisions are taken, distinguishing between the 'operational environment' – which they posit as objective reality – and the 'psychological environment' – which they hold to be subjective and under the influence of a myriad of perceptual biases and cognitive stimuli.[12] Foreign policy decision makers take decisions on the basis of their psychological environment, relying upon perceptions as a guide, rather than any cold weighing of objective facts. Harold and Margaret Sprout believed that the accompanying gap between the 'operational environment' and the 'psychological environment' within which decision makers act introduced significant distortions into foreign policy making with important implications for foreign policy as a whole. This division which they set out proved to be a defining feature of the emerging critique of rationalist accounts of decision making, opening up an examination of the impact that psychological and cognitive factors have on the minds of decision makers.

Richard Snyder and colleagues took this insight further, pointing out that it was inaccurate to ascribe decision making to the autonomous unitary entity known as the state.[13] In their view, the 'black box of foreign policy decision making' needed to be opened up so that one could both recognize the actual complexity underlying decisions (which includes individual biases and bureaucratic processes) and develop a better analysis of foreign policy itself. The result was a focus on the actors, processes and ultimately the structures of foreign policy decision making within the state as sources of explanation for foreign policy. A key contribution made by Snyder was to emphasize the 'definition of the situation' by foreign policy makers.[14] What this notion sought to capture was the centrality of decision makers – and with it their subjective biases – in defining, assessing and interpreting foreign policy events. Human agency, with all its foibles, was in this way reasserted to be at the core of international politics.[15]

For these critics of rationality, foreign policy decision makers do not act in a purely rational manner that conforms to the core assumptions of realism and public choice theory. At best, foreign policy decision makers could be said to operate within the framework of the information available to them and make decisions on that limited basis. Moreover, decision makers are subject also to other influences, such as their perceptions, pre-existing beliefs or prejudices and cognitive limitations on handling information, which introduce further distortions to the process. Much of the substance of this latter critique against rationality as a source of foreign policy decision making was made by the behaviourists in their work on individual decision makers. Critics of rationality believe that attempts at rational foreign policy decision making are misguided and even potentially dangerous for states.

The role of perception

In dividing the setting of foreign policy decision making between the 'operational' and 'psychological' environments, Harold and Margaret Sprout opened up the possibility of FPA scholars investigating the interior lives of individual foreign policy makers. Psychology, especially the work on perception and cognition, became a critical resource for understanding these dynamics inherent in the decision making conducted by individuals. Underlying this approach is cognitive psychology's general insights on human behaviour which suggest human beings prefer simplicity to complexity, seek consistency over ambiguity, are poor estimators of probability and are loss averse.[16] These fundamental attributes play a critical role in shaping the foreign policy decision-making process.

Robert Jervis produced one of the most influential studies in this area on the role of 'misperception' in foreign policy decisions, which he says stems from the fact that leaders make foreign policy based upon their perceptions rather than the actual 'operational environment'. His studies demonstrate that individual leaders draw upon a personalized understanding of history in their efforts to both interpret international events and devise appropriate responses to them.[17] These interpretations are rooted in a relatively stable set of beliefs which, when coupled with the cognitive drive for consistency, produce a deliberate (if unintended) reinforcing of the leader's evolving foreign policy prescription and the underlying beliefs upon which they are based.[18] For Kenneth Boulding, this suggests that foreign policy decisions are largely the product of the 'images' that individual leaders have of other countries or leaders and, therefore, are based upon stereotypes, biases and other subjective sources that interfere with their ability to conduct rational foreign policy.[19] All these scholars see leadership as bringing its particular experience and outlook, perhaps shaped by individual and societal prejudices or media imagery, to the foreign policy process and thus introducing distortions in 'the definition of the situation'.

Within the realm of foreign policy decision making itself, the apparent symmetry between two potential choices posited by rationalism is subject to underlying psychological biases. The recognition by psychologists that human beings are loss averse, that is, they give greater weight to actions that potentially could stave off loss in relation to actions that might produce gain, provides insight into the consistency with which decision makers pursue 'preservationist' outcomes – producing sub-optimal choices – within game theory. While this relative weighting of the fear of loss compared to gain is accounted for to some extent by rational choice scholars, the broader point is that it suggests that perceptual factors have a primordial hold on the mechanism of choice. Concurrently, there is well-founded empirical evidence that while decision makers persistently ascribe purposeful rationality to the decisions of other actors, they allow for a host of externalities as sources of influence over their own decision-making processes. This belief or 'fundamental attribution error' leads to a pattern of under-estimation of the constraints affecting 'opponents' in relation to oneself and contributes to distortions in foreign policy decision making.[20]

The role of cognition

Another dimension of the psychological approach that affects foreign policy is cognition. Cognition, the process by which humans select and process information from the world around them, introduces important problems to the decision-making process. For instance, the sheer volume of possible information that could significantly impact upon a particular foreign policy and the patent inability of an individual to recognise on process it successfully is a well-known problem. Indeed, the limits that cognition – when coupled to the role of perception – imposes on a rational account of foreign policy are such that it is difficult to describe these decisions as anything but the product of an incomplete (and therefore unsatisfactory) process.

Cognitive consistency is a crucial concept for FPA scholars working on decision-making dynamics. The impulse to seek out and reinforce the existing beliefs of decision makers is a fundamental cognitive drive for human beings. Jervis's investigation of 'cognitive consistency' points out that foreign policy makers habitually screen out the disruptive effects by finding a logical way of incorporating them into the rationale for a given foreign policy choice.[21] Building upon these insights, other behaviourist scholars have highlighted the distortions to rational foreign policy imposed by the search for cognitive consistency by individual leaders. Leon Festinger's concept of 'cognitive dissonance', that is, the effort by which a decision maker deliberately excludes new or contradictory information, in order to maintain his/her existing image or cognitive map, is one example of this.[22] Rosati's work on 'schema theory', however, suggests that these accounts of cognitive consistency are too rigid.[23] Cognitive theorists assume that individual decision makers are fixated on maintaining a well-integrated belief system and that this is both resistant to change as well as serving as a singular source for foreign policy choice. Schema theory posits a much more fragmented depiction of beliefs, which are said to be understood better as isolated repositories of knowledge, allowing for the inconsistency that characterizes their application to foreign policy decision making. The role of learning in foreign policy, including the drive to use history as a basis for decision making, is an expression of this dynamic process (see Chapter 7 for further details).

Given the desire to produce a predictive science of foreign policy within FPA, attempts have been made to put these insights into a workable framework which captures a leader's beliefs in a systemic way. According to Alexander George, the international environment is filtered by decision makers through their own 'operational code', that is, a set of rules and perceptions that have previously been established within their minds and which are used to assess new situations and develop policy responses to them.[24] Robert Axelrod suggests that this interrelationship between individual leaders and their environments can best be explained through the development of a 'cognitive map' that combines perception, prejudice and an understanding of 'historical lessons' and applies these to the task of decision making.[25] His research findings suggest, moreover, that foreign policy makers tend towards those policy choices that involve the fewest trade-offs, not necessarily the 'best' or 'optimal' policies that the rational choice theorists would have us believe, but the ones that involve the path of least resistance. Indeed, some characterize this sub-optimal decision making as 'satisficing', that is, the decision maker's impulse to choose a policy option that addresses the immediate pressures and concerns rather than weighing the merits of a given policy.[26]

The role of personality

In addition to perception and cognition, FPA scholars have tried to assess the impact of a leader's personality on foreign policy. They note that different leaders bring their own biases to office and – this is most evident in the removal of one leader and the installation of another – can exercise dramatically different influences over their countries' foreign policies. For example, scholars point to John F. Kennedy's inexperience and youth compared to Nikita Khrushchev, as a factor that played into the latter's decision to deploy Soviet missiles in Cuba in 1962.[27] Ironically, in another mark of the force of personality on foreign policy, General Charles de Gaulle cited Kennedy's willingness to tolerate the hostile Castro regime within striking distance of the US in the aftermath of the Cuban missile crisis as a key causal factor in his decision to pull France out of NATO (North Atlantic Treaty

Organization) and embark on an independent French nuclear weapons programme.[28] De Gaulle reasoned that if Kennedy would not use force against an obvious military threat to the US population then the American president would not be willing to support the use of US troops in defence of French interests. Finally, Tony Blair's commitment to the 2003 Iraq invasion has been tied by some scholars to his 'messianic' personality.[29] Psychological profiling of leaders, analysing the origins of their patterns of behaviour as a clue to their possible actions, has become an important preoccupation for FPA scholars.[30] All these individualistic and deeply personal elements are said to affect leadership and ultimately foreign policy outcomes.

In their study of personality, Irving Janis and Leon Mann introduce a 'motivational' model of foreign policy decision making that emphasizes the fact that leaders are emotional beings seeking to resolve internal decisional conflict.[31] The role of emotions is most pronounced in a crisis and at this point stress intervenes, causing a lack of ability to abstract and tolerate ambiguity and an increased tendency towards aggressive behaviour. Tunnel vision, fixation on single solutions to the exclusion of all others, may also ensue under these trying circumstances as leaders struggle to manage the complexity of decisions.[32] According to some scholars, those leaders who are more highly motivated by the pursuit of power have a propensity for confrontational foreign policy, while those inclined towards greater interpersonal trust display more conciliatory forms of foreign policy.[33]

Another manifestation of personality in foreign policy is the particular leadership style adopted by the key foreign policy actor. According to Orbovich and Molnar, four different cognitive leadership styles are possible, from systemic (rationalist, cost-benefit calculation), speculative (context-oriented), judicial (task-oriented) to intuitive (relies on non-rational approach, 'hunches').[34] Management of the decision-making process in foreign policy, be it seeking emotional reinforcement from an advisory group or using the group to affirm the leader's decision through forced consensus, is a reflection of the emotional disposition of the foreign policy decision maker.[35]

All these psychological factors are brought directly to bear on the foreign policy decision maker's assessment of the relative risk of a particular choice. Prospect theory suggests that when foreign policy decision makers perceive their setting to be one of gain they become risk averse, seeking to hold on to their attainments. Conversely, when foreign policy decision makers perceive themselves to be operating in a setting of loss they become risk takers, gambling on achieving gains through the pursuit of high-risk actions.[36] These situational (or 'domain') settings provide a context in which the rationality of the decision-making process is maintained in procedural terms, but is fatally compromised by subjective assessments of the situation faced by the foreign policy decision maker.

The role of the group

The same human psychological and cognitive limitations which challenge the rational actor model of decision making apply also to groups. Group decision-making structures, which are put in place in order to broaden the information base, provide alternative sources of analysis and experience – in other words to combat some of the perceptual misconceptions and cognitive shortcomings that arise in individual decision making – and introduce a new set of problems. Janis's investigation of foreign policy making by groups concludes that they suffer from 'group think', that is to say individuals tend to seek to maintain consensus when operating in a group even at the expense of promoting their own particular (and possibly more sensible) perspective on an issue under discussion.[37] Through this process of concurrency seeking behaviour by group members, the objectively best (or 'optimal') decision to a given foreign policy dilemma can become diluted or even abandoned as individuals strive to come up with a common group position on how to address a specific foreign policy challenge.

Considerable scholarship has been devoted to ameliorating the worst effects of group think, including restructuring groups periodically and reviewing decisions under consideration. George proposes a number of measures to combat this tendency, including the imposition of a devil's advocate to question pending decisions and rotation of leaders within smaller groups, but the fact remains that under circumstances where time is an issue, such as is the case in foreign policy crises, the impulse towards seeking consensus for sub-optimal policy positions is strong.[38] Other scholars have sought to go 'beyond group think' and re-examine the phenomenon in light of new data and insights. Stern and Sundelius, for instance, suggest that a key case examined by Janis, that of the Bay of Pigs fiasco, is better explained by 'new group syndrome' and an absence of assertive leadership than the pathologies associated with group think.[39]

Critiques of the foreign policy decision-making approach

The psychological approach in many respects is a devastating one for proponents of rationality in foreign policy. Nevertheless its limitations as an interpretive tool in FPA have become evident to many working in the discipline. Holsti, for example, ultimately seeks to downplay the significance of psychological factors in foreign policy by stressing the importance of the operational environment as determining foreign policy independent of the psychological environment. He says foreign policy cannot be usefully explained if one does not take into account several levels of analysis in addition to the individual level (where considerations of perception, cognition and personality do matter), namely bureaucratic constraints, domestic influences and the external environment.[40] Moreover, the stock of images, perceptions and ideology identified by FPA scholars are not the products of individuals, but rather emerge out of society (they are 'socially constructed') and therefore it is not especially relevant to focus on individuals alone. It would be more meaningful to focus on the social context within which they operate.

Also, the importance of personality in foreign policy is discounted by some scholars. Steve Smith's study of the Iran hostage crisis suggests that personality is not as significant as the actual role assumed by individuals holding positions of authority.[41] We explore this issue further in Chapter 3. Others point to the difficulty of measuring the degree of input of psychological factors on foreign policy outcomes – can one really ascribe the decision of Charles de Gaulle to pull France out of Algeria, to formative events in his background, and, if so, why were they any more important than the social, economic and security reasons for taking action? Overall, personality – as well as perception and cognition – can usefully contribute to explain aspects of the process of choice in foreign policy, but cannot serve as the sole or overarching explanation.

Psychological approaches in FPA provide a window on decision making that enriches our understanding of the myriad of possible influences on the foreign policy choices made by leaders. In many ways, it could be argued that the work of FPA scholars on perception and cognition anticipate the insights provided by constructivists working in IR theory a generation later.[42] There are distinctive differences, for instance, the focus on the individual construction of reality in FPA contrasts with the collective construction of reality which features in constructivism, reflecting their differing emphases on the role of structure and agency. Debates within constructivism centre around the role of social norms versus discourses as key processes in formulating inter-subjective meanings which have implications for the focus of research in FPA. With respect to the former, the concept of 'strategic social rationality' as applied by norms entrepreneurs conforms more readily to the broader framework of rationality adopted by FPA, especially as reformulated through ideas such as 'bounded rationality'. At the same time, the commitment to positivism inherent in the formative division between the 'objective' and 'subjective' environments of foreign policy decision making, produces a barrier to FPA scholars fully embracing constructivist notions of 'inter-subjectivity'.

Elucidating the limitations of the decision-making formulation from a different angle, scholars have emphasized the neglect of foreign policy implementation as an area of study in FPA.[43] Revisiting Charles Lindblom's celebrated critique of the rationalist depiction of decision making by scholars of public administration provides further insight into the relationship between foreign policy formulation and its implementation. He points out that empirical studies demonstrate that decisions are not, as rationalists would have it, made in a linear top-down fashion but rather through a 'root and branch' approach.[44] What this suggests is that the implementing agents themselves – distant from the policy makers in spatial, emotional and often a geographic sense as well – exercise considerable sway over foreign policy. They attribute meaning to foreign policy and through their responsibility for implementation they affect the manner in which these foreign policy directives are actually operationalized. In so doing, implementing agents have a direct impact on foreign policy, feeding back into the process, thereby affecting the perceptions and choices of top-level foreign policy makers. This feedback process is generally seen to be an imperfect one by participants and carries with it the possibilities of exacerbating the distorting impact of psychology and cognition. The decision-making literature in FPA has not developed a sufficient understanding of the interpretive and operational impact implementing agencies have on foreign policy. This calls for a kind of 'sub-altern' form of analysis of foreign policy decision making rooted in unpacking the relatively unexplored motives, methods and actions of foreign policy implementing agents rather than the perpetual focus on the policy makers. In our view this would do much to enhance the analytical purchase of decision-making theory.

Reconciling rational and non-rational approaches: bounded rationality, cybernetics and poliheuristics

Efforts to rehabilitate rationality as a source for foreign policy decision making have resulted in a number of innovative approaches that attempt to incorporate the insights and criticisms levelled against it. Herbert Simon's work (although he is not an IR scholar, but an economist) suggests that while decision makers cannot achieve pure rationality, they nonetheless conduct themselves along the lines of 'procedural' rationality when faced with a particular policy dilemma. Foreign policy makers, therefore, operate within the framework of what Simon calls 'bounded rationality', that is, they act rationally within the context of partial information and other limitations placed on decisions.[45]

John Steinbruner, responding to the general critique on rationality, the problematic of group decision making and the issues raised by the bureaucratic politics model, introduced what he called a cybernetic processing approach to foreign policy. He posits that there are three paradigms in decision making – analytical (or rational), cybernetic and cognitive – and that an integration of the last two more accurately captures the actual process of decision making and the foibles of individual and group actors.[46]

Alex Mintz proposed another way of reconciling the critique against rationality in foreign policy decision making while maintaining much of the substance of rational choice approaches.[47] Mintz proposed the 'poliheuristic method', declaring that foreign policy decision making is best understood as a two-stage process. In the first step the non-rational elements governing decision making hold, in particular considerations of what is politically possible by the leader of the state, and the menu of policy options is developed on that basis. These are 'non-compensatory' choices, that is to say, selection is not subject to trade-off in terms of the calculation of utility (costs versus benefits) as the domain in which decisions are considered is situated firmly within the realm of the decision maker's domestic environment. Once courses of action that are not politically palatable or attainable, such as surrendering sovereign territory in response to a foreign ultimatum, are discarded, the second step of decision making occurs. In this stage, policy options are introduced and selected in a rational manner that conforms to the rules of public choice theory, namely that foreign policy decisions are driven primarily by a search for the maximization of utility within a particular framework.

The strength of Mintz's approach is that it attempts to account for the variations in outcomes through integration of the impact of non-rational factors on that process and a systemic and parsimonious approach to handling the multifaceted features of foreign policy decision making. At the same time, poliheuristic theory leaves open issues such as the nature and impact of a given decision-making structure, which essentially is depicted by Mintz as unitary, on choice, as well as more conventional concerns associated with rational choice theory around preference formation as given or 'exogenous'. Moreover, it is difficult to claim that the singular focus on 'political survivability' at the first stage of decision making adequately addresses the concerns raised by some of rationality's most trenchant critiques: rather poliheuristic theory seems to dismiss matters such as cognition and psychological factors in favour of this mono-clausal depiction of the sources of agency. One could take the position that domestic politics is *the* core non-rational concern that is paramount for all decision makers and, since it involves the leader's perceptions of threat, can serve as a proxy for the impact of cognition on the process, but scholars working in this area do not assert this: in fact, some have sought to expand the number of non-compensatory dimensions.[48] And, finally, while poliheuristic theory is predicated on assessing risk – political risk in its most explicit form in stage one of the decision-making process – it nonetheless does not account for differing frames of reference for decision making and their impact on risk assessment as outlined above, in prospect theory. Despite these concerns, poliheuristic theory represents a compelling attempt to revive and expand the role of modified forms of rational choice in formulating a theory of foreign policy decision making.

Conclusion

What is clear from the above analysis is that a purely rational account of foreign policy decision making cannot hold up against the various criticisms, whether psychological or empirical in content. At the same time, the durability of rationality as a means of analysing foreign policy continues and, in part, reflects the willingness of FPA scholars to accept the basic tenets of criticism, but also their reluctance to abandon the methodology of public choice. This commitment to retaining features of rationality, albeit somewhat reduced in scope and ambition, is integral to FPA's focus on developing a predictive understanding of the decision-making process.

It should be pointed out that the influence of rationality is more widespread than in the realm of FPA theory debates alone. Rational analyses of foreign policy underlie much of our average interpretation of international events and we are making assumptions about the unitary nature of decision makers when we talk, for example, about 'French foreign policy' without accounting for different influences on decision making within governments. Thus, while criticisms of rationality remain both powerful and valid, its assumptions still play an important part in much of our day-to-day understanding of foreign policy.

As this chapter shows, the relationship between the decision maker, the state and the structure of the international system is complex and it can be argued that the utility of such concepts as misperception in explaining different types of foreign policy depend as much on the characteristics of the state, the issue being addressed and the type of policy being formulated, as on the leader's cognitive constraints. Since, arguably, all foreign policy decisions are the product of the foreign policy institutions within which decisions are taken, there is a compelling case for broadening the focus to include institutional procedures and bureaucracies. In keeping with this insight, in Chapter 3 we examine the impact of these organizations on the foreign policy process.

3   Bureaucracies and foreign policy

Introduction

Chapter 2 looked at different approaches to examining foreign policy decision making. These approaches directly challenge the realist assumption that foreign policy is a rational process, producing outcomes that correspond neatly to the initial preference-orderings of states. Another core assumption of realism that the state is a rational, unitary actor, was challenged in the early 1960s. A growing literature has examined how state bureaucracies impact on foreign policy, highlighting the fragmented and often institutionally driven nature of foreign policy making and implementation. Chapter 3 examines this literature with the aim of exploring its implications for the making and implementation of foreign policy. In our view other works on FPA, similar to our own, which try to account for and advance the field of FPA, have not captured this debate in its entirety.[1] They focus mainly on Allison's work and the initial critiques it generated while overlooking more recent refinements and proposals for new directions for work on bureaucracies and foreign policy. Thus, we think an up-to-date account is useful to enable development of the interest in FPA of the connection between bureaucracies and foreign policy.

Developing a theory of bureaucratic politics

In the early 1960s a group of scholars – e.g. Neustadt, Huntington, Crozier, Schilling and his colleagues – became interested in the impact of bureaucracies on foreign policy. This literature, harbinger of bureaucratic politics theory, provides empirical insights into how the administrative structures of government affect foreign policy. The findings are somewhat controversial in arguing that the stances adopted derive not only from the merits of the proposed foreign policy, but also from the foreign policy makers' positions in their respective government bureaucracies. Different institutional settings mean officials and politicians viewed foreign policy issues through different prisms resulting in distinctly different views.[2] This evolving body of literature has converged around a central proposition: decision-making *processes* determine the *content of* foreign policy. Accordingly, political leadership is portrayed in terms of the ability to persuade and to achieve consensus among policy makers. From this vantage point foreign policy reflects 'the necessities of the conditions in which it is forged – what is required to obtain agreement – [as much] as it does the merits of that policy'.[3]

In the 1970s, another group of scholars developed these empirical insights into a theory. This group was committed to the development of IR, and the study of foreign policy in particular, into what Kuhn terms 'normal science – the activity of articulating theory, determining significant facts, and matching facts with theory'.[4] The contours of this debate are defined in Graham Allison's seminal work on the Cuban missile crisis, *The Essence of Decision-Making*. Allison challenges what he refers to as the rational policy model, which 'attempts to understand happenings as the more or less purposive acts of unified national governments'.[5] Allison and his followers argue that although in many instances the rational policy model may be useful, it neglects the role of bureaucracy in determining foreign policy.[6] Allison proposed two alternative models to address this intellectual lacuna: the organizational process model, or Model II, and the bureaucratic politics model (BPM), or Model III. However, the explanatory power of Model II proved to be limited, particularly in relation to foreign policy *change* and innovation. In addition, critics claimed that it was not clear whether Model III was separate from or merely an extension of Model II.[7] Eventually, the organizational politics model was collapsed into the BPM, 'relegating the organizational process to the status of "constraints" within the bureaucratic model paradigm'.[8]

The BPM explains foreign policy in terms of a conglomerate of large, bureaucratic organizations and political actors. The former are relevant to foreign policy on two counts. First, they generate outputs that structure the situations in which policy makers take decisions. These outputs include: the information bureaucracies provide to governments; the foreign policy alternatives presented for government to choose from; and the standard operating procedures (SOPs) which shape how foreign policy decisions ultimately are implemented.[9] Second, bureaucracies tend to develop common attitudes and shared images. These conventional attitudes and images play a role in framing how a particular foreign policy issue or event is perceived by foreign policy makers. Bureaucracies often will employ the prism of their common attitudes and shared images to study the implications of a foreign policy event for policy making. For example, when considering a security issue, the Treasury tends to focus on the budgetary implications, the Department of Defence on the repercussions for national security, while the Foreign Office most likely focuses on the diplomatic and international political ramifications.[10]

Bureaucracies also derive influence over foreign policy from their positions in the power-sharing structure comprising state and government, in which these large organizations and political actors have individual interests. These interests include enhancing the bureaucratic influence in the domestic political arena, augmenting their resources, furthering their ability to fulfil their stated missions and maintaining morale among their personnel.[11] Those interests, which reflect the organizational health and position of a given bureaucracy within government, often may not coincide with the 'national interest'. In fact, because each bureaucracy manipulates foreign policy in the direction that corresponds to *its* particular interests, bureaucratic considerations may override the national interest.[12] Allison and Halperin explain that the BPM tries to capture this complex dynamic, demonstrating that foreign policy is messier than the rational policy model would concede:

[The] bureaucratic model sees no unitary actor but rather many actors as players -- players who focus not on a single strategic issue but on many diverse intra-national problems as well. Players choose in terms of no consistent set of strategic objectives but rather according to various conceptions of national security, organizational, domestic, and personal interests. Players make governmental decision not by a single rational choice, but by pulling and hauling.[13]

The approach outlined by the BPM not only seeks to explain the foreign policy of individual states, it has implications also for the relations between states. Whilst the rational policy model accounts for the interaction between states in terms of a 'competition between two purposive individuals' the BPM explanation 'focuses primarily on the political processes internal to each state'.[14] Accordingly, foreign policy actions matter only to the extent that they influence the domestic struggles within nationally bounded decision-making apparatuses. In this view, foreign policy is depicted as the unintended result of a bargaining process involving the principal participants.[15] The important question, then, is not why did this state do X, as realist logic would imply, but rather why did X happen?[16]

Initial critiques

The powerful theoretical and analytical purchase of the BPM has generated a rich empirical research agenda: from foreign policy crises and weapons acquisitions, through alliance politics and arms control, to US military in Vietnam.[17] At the same time, the BPM has provoked fierce criticism.[18] Stephen Krasner, for instance, brands the BPM as misleading in so far as it obscures the power of the president in the making and implementation of foreign policy in the US. Krasner also argues that the BPM is dangerous because it implies that bureaucracies have taken over the foreign policy making apparatus. In line with this logic, unaccounted-for bureaucracies rather than the elected officials are responsible for the actions of government. By extension, the notion of responsible decision makers is rendered meaningless. Moreover, holding elected officials to account for their actions via elections or, when the case arises, the judiciary, is futile. Herein lies the danger of the BPM: it undermines the assumptions of democratic politics. Finally, argues Krasner, the BPM offers leaders an excuse for their failure and an opportunity for scholars to account for those failures.

On these grounds Krasner vehemently objects to the BPM. He insists that politicians, in particular the US president, can make choices and value judgements and control the bureaucracies at their disposal, particularly in the foreign policy realm. After all, the president chooses most of the key players and sets many of the rules. Moreover, these players will often have shared mindsets and images that will dominate foreign policy making. Therefore, they should be held accountable for their actions.[19] The analytical framework underpinning BPM has also been criticized. Art, for instance, argues that the BPM makes broad claims about the impact of organizations and the domestic struggle between the principal players. However, the model does not specify under what circumstances, and in relation to which issue areas, will organizations and domestic struggles have the greatest impact on foreign policy formulation and its implementation. Similarly, the BPM does not account accurately for how and to what extent bureaucracies during the process of implementation will subvert the government's foreign policy intent.[20]

There are also some methodological concerns. Freedman argues, for example, that Allison's distinction between the rational policy model and the BPM is informed by a false dichotomy between logic and politics. This leads the BPM model to identify alternative, mutually exclusive routes to policy, 'recognized by whether or not actual disagreement is observed'. Freedman argues that through this prism, the BPM and the rational policy model are no longer distinct foreign policy models. Rather, they are situated at the extreme ends of one continuum. One extreme captures those instances when governments approach a given foreign policy issue from a position of agreement, involving investigation of issues where the rational choice model is particularly appropriate. The other end of the spectrum captures contexts best examined through the lens of BPM and involves situations where disagreement underpins government's formulation and implementation of a given foreign policy issue. However, the BPM is regarded as being the more deficient of the two since it tends to employ a very narrow concept of the political aspect of foreign policy where politics is reduced to an intrusion by the parochial preoccupations, ambitions and suspicions of the people responsible for making foreign policy and their bureaucracies.

The BPM methodology is also criticized for its over-reliance on the 'game' metaphor. The game metaphor has significant explanatory purchase for depicting the present, providing a detailed picture of the mix of motivations, assumptions, talents intricacies, plans and accidents that constitute foreign policy. However, the analytical gains accrued from focusing on bureaucratic infighting are undercut by the BPM's lack of attention to non-bureaucratic foreign policy determinants: from cognitive factors, values, and the type of state in which bureaucrats operate (democratic/authoritarian), through the impact of interest groups and congress, to the public.[21] This critique underscores that taking account of the effect of non-bureaucratic factors on foreign policy makes the *relative* impact of bureaucracies seem less significant than is assumed by the BPM.

The politics/logic false dichotomy, the game metaphor problem, the omission of non-bureaucratic foreign policy determinants are not the only critiques of the BPM methodology. There is also a preoccupation with the problems associated with how the BPM employs the theories of the *firm* to the analysis of government decision making, and two issues in particular. First, the goals of financial actors – e.g. profit, sales, production – are different from the ends pursued by bureaucracies in the foreign policy realm. Second, it is easier to measure the success or failure of firms (based on profit or loss) than to evaluate foreign policy. This questions the extent to which the assumptions underpinning the theories of the firm can be applied to bureaucracies involved in the formulation and implementation of foreign policy.[22]

Refining the theory of bureaucratic politics

The charged debate promoted by the BPM has led to productive discussions on how to address its deficiencies without completely losing its essence. As already noted in reference to Krasner's work, critiques challenge the BPM understanding of the relationship in government organizations between human agency and bureaucratic impact. Specifically, the account provided by the BPM assigns too much power to the impact of bureaucracies on individual actions. Through the prism of BPM individuals emerge merely as puppets whose actions and decisions derive from the vested interests of their bureaucracies and SOPs. In other words, the individual becomes the personification of the bureaucracy, its vested interests and its SOPs. Hollis and Smith substantially improve on the rather mechanistic view of individuals made subordinate to the logic of their bureaucracies.[23] Their account is predicated on the idea that individuals have a role in bureaucracy, based on the expectations and accountability deriving from their jobs, their duties, spheres of authority and responsibilities.

The role of individuals is not consistent. At times bureaucrats and politicians are required to perform the dual role of office holder *and* who they are as individuals. For example, when Tony Blair discussed the possibility of the UK invading Iraq he was not involved *solely* as prime minister: he was simultaneously a self-confessed churchgoer and a morally concerned human being.[24] This suggests a potential conflict between his role as prime minister and his role as an individual. Bureaucrats and politicians generally judge themselves and are judged by others, according to how they perform as office holders rather than on the basis of their private integrity. Arguably, therefore, the role of office holder supersedes, though does not nullify, the role of the individual.

These roles, as well as being inconsistent, are also not static. As situations develop, the expectations of a given office holder may change, affecting the role being assumed. Such change occurs despite the bureaucratic determinants – for example, the organization's vested interest and SOP – remaining constant. Finally, an office holder's roles are not reducible to the individual position within the bureaucracy because, in part at least, this role defines the relationships with other 'role players', holding office in other bureaucracies. These 'external' role players will condemn individual office holders who fail to meet their expectations and, correspondingly, will applaud them when they do. In exhibiting inconsistency, fluidity and dependence on the actions of external actors, roles are not reducible to the individual's position deriving from the SOP of the bureaucracy and its interests. Roles possess a relative autonomy from the influence exerted by bureaucratic elements. Hence, they are crucial for defining what policy makers can and cannot do in their job roles. Chapter 7, which discusses foreign policy and change, examines this issue in further detail.

Hollis and Smith were not alone in questioning the BPM's depiction of the relationship between human agency and bureaucratic impact. As noted earlier, the BPM holds that the impact of bureaucracies is so strong as to *oblige* the head of the executive to bargain with members of his/her own administration. Critique of this aspect of the BPM raises the obvious question of why bargaining should be necessary since the head of the executive appoints the top officials, has the power to dismiss them and has substantial formal authority, especially on foreign affairs, to order subordinates to perform what he/she wants.[25]

In this light it would seem not a foregone conclusion that the head of the executive is required to bargain with subordinates. It is arguable that proponents of the BPM are interested in understanding *the degree to which* the head of the executive is required to bargain. Much depends on the extent to which these subordinates can muster support from *outside* the executive (parliament/congress) to support a view that may differ from that of the head of the executive. The greater the support that can be mustered outside the executive the more fiercely the head of the executive will have to bargain to get his/her view implemented, and vice versa. Nevertheless, the degree to which the head of the executive is obliged to bargain does not derive solely from the level of external support that subordinates receive from outside the executive. It depends also on whether key players within an administration/government, whose views diverge from those of the head of the executive, can form a unified opposition to counter the head of the executive's view. A strong coalition that supported the head of the executive would probably be able to resist dissent, even if supported by elements outside the executive.

Another factor influencing the degree to which the head of the executive will be required to bargain is information asymmetry with subordinates. Ostensibly, the greater the asymmetry in favour of the subordinates the more the head of the executive will be required to bargain, and vice versa.[26] However, there are measures that the head of the executive can take to mitigate the effects created by information asymmetries. For instance, heads of state often will employ a wide communication network, beyond the state apparatus, that alerts them to potential problems and provides essential information on them. This information renders the head of the executive better placed than the BPM would suggest to deal with information asymmetries vis-à-vis subordinates. In addition, the head of the executive usually (though not always) has the time and opportunity to study the topics deemed to be important and to reduce information asymmetry with subordinates. A third factor related to the need to bargain, is how the hierarchy within government bureaucracies affects politics and decision making. The design of bureaucracies thrusts some issues to the surface while marginalizing others. Since decision makers inevitably are more concerned about certain issues, the hierarchical configuration within a bureaucracy is crucial in terms of the ability of the actors to set agendas and determine whether or not the head of the executive needs to bargain. For example, a prime minister may not bring an issue to the vote unless certain of enough support for it to pass.[27]

Work on the 'role' of foreign policy and 'bargaining' enhances our understanding of the relationship between human agency and bureaucracies *within* executive decision-making units. Further advances in the debate on the BPM have enhanced our understanding of the relationship *between* the executive and bureaucracies. Rosati's work is extremely useful for exploring this issue.[28] He argues that the first phase of the debate on BPM was unhelpful in focusing on whether the executive *or* the bureaucracy has greater influence over foreign policy. A more useful approach is to recognize that different circumstances mean that different actors exert varying degrees of influence on foreign policy. The executive is expected to be most heavily involved when the foreign policy issue is most critical for the national interest. Ascertaining the importance of a foreign policy issue in part is a rational process involving prioritization and goal setting. However, it is not wholly rational because it depends also and significantly on the context of the foreign policy. By context we mean the level of prior planning required to reach a decision, the time available for deliberation and choice, and the values informing the decision makers' evaluation of foreign policy issues. Thus, the impact of the executive is expected to be experienced most strongly in a crisis situation – involving surprise, short time and perception of a high level of threat.[29] The bureaucracy, in its turn, will dominate in the context of moderately important foreign policy issues where the executive's influence is expected to be low. Finally, if a foreign policy issue is seen as low priority, we should expect local dominance, with low level of executive and bureaucratic involvement overall. In these circumstances, individual bureaucrats will be more visible than the bureaucracy.

Each of these scenarios – executive dominance, bureaucratic influence, local dominance – constitutes a decision-making structure. Because governments are required to deal simultaneously with a multiplicity of foreign policy issues, no one decision-making structure will prevail at any given moment. Rather, all three decision-making structures will operate simultaneously, with one most dominant (although not totally eclipsing the other two).[30] This formulation addresses some of the critiques raised earlier with reference to Art's work. In particular, his concern that the BPM is not sufficiently specific about when and under what circumstances the influence of organizations in foreign policy will prevail.

New directions

With the benefit of hindsight scholars can not only refine particular aspects of the debate on BPM – for example, human agency vs. the impact of bureaucracy, the relationship between the executive and state bureaucracies. Students of bureaucratic politics can also assess how Allison and colleagues' work fares in terms of the empirical work it spawned and theoretical developments in the field. In this connection, Hammond and Bendor's re-evaluation of Allison's theoretical framework is insightful. These authors scrutinize the rational policy model, Model I, arguing that, in important respects, Allison's depiction of the rational policy model is unclear. For example, the model should be more explicit about whether it assumes that actors pursue one or a number of foreign policy goals simultaneously. In fact, Hammond and Bendor argue forcefully that it should be assumed that any actor would opt for the latter and that rational action theory would label actors pursuing only one goal monomaniacal and treat them as *irrational*. However, Allison's formulation is equivocal on this issue. Another area where Allison's rational policy model is vague is whether decision making occurs within one or multiple timeframes. This issue is crucial because if it is assumed that foreign policy making occurs within one timeframe, then the inference is that a given state considers its actions in terms of its *short-term effects*. However, if this assumption is relaxed to allow foreign policy making to be considered as an activity that occurs within multiple timeframes, then the inference is that the action of a given state is considered in terms of its *long-term effects*. Long-term effects could include a country's reputation for firmness, for resolve, support of allies and compliance with agreements.

Hammond and Bendor, in addition to accusing Allison of lack of clarity about whether actors pursue one or multiple goals, and about the timeframe within which foreign policy occurs, critique Allison for overlooking certain issues crucial for constructing the rational policy model. For instance, they accuse him of not addressing the problem posed by uncertainty for rational decision making. When Allison's work was first published the issue of uncertainty had already been dealt with extensively by IR theory, especially within the realist tradition. Its palpable implications for foreign policy mean that the issue of uncertainty is pertinent for Allison's conception of rational policy. For instance, during the Cuban missile crisis uncertainty about the weather conditions influenced the military's decisions related to the feasibility of a surgical attack. More importantly, uncertainty within the US administration about the Soviet's motives produced competing explanations about why the missiles had been sited in Cuba in the first place. On these three issues – of not specifying whether actors pursue a single or multiple goals, whether foreign policy occurs within one or multiple timeframes, and uncertainty – Hammond and Bendor render Allison's rational policy model *too simple*. They argue persuasively that Allison constructed a straw man using the model to vindicate his alternative account of the Cuban missile crisis. Their critique raises a methodological and analytical bar that contemporary theory of bureaucratic politics is required to clear before it can claim greater explanatory purchase than the rational policy model.[31]

Contemporary critiques criticize Allison's depiction of the rational policy model and also scrutinize the assumptions underpinning Allison's formulations of Models II and III, the organizational and bureaucratic models. David Welch's work, based on cross-national comparisons, a review of the empirical work generated by BPM and meticulous reading of Allison's work, provides an important contribution.[32] Welch argues that the evidence generated by the vast body of empirical research using Allison's models is too equivocal to corroborate the key hypotheses underpinning Model II. These are that existing organizational routines limit the range of available options in a given situation, resist change, determine the course of implementation and systematically induce instrumental irrationalities in state behaviour. In fact research shows that ultimately *different* effects are generated by *bureaucratic routines* in foreign policy decision making and implementation and, therefore, cannot constitute a useful analytical category for theory. Similarly, there is no firm evidence from empirical research that vindicates the key assumptions underpinning Model III – that players' preferences, perceptions and influence correlate with their bureaucratic positions; foreign policy is the result of pull and push among the players. Given these ambivalences, argues Welch, the BPM can no longer aspire to be a *theory* of foreign policy.

Welch's argument seems plausible because for the BPM to become a theory of foreign policy would require bureaucratic politics being treated as an independent variable. In reality, however, for a number of reasons, the impact of bureaucratic politics on foreign policy varies. Earlier we noted, with reference to Rosati's work, that the particular issue has a strong impact on whether bureaucrats or the executive has the greater influence on foreign policy. Other factors also matter. For example, the more the bureaucrats are able to enlist ministers at cabinet level to support their turf battles, the greater will be the impact of bureaucratic politics on policy making. In other instances, politicians enlist the bureaucrats to promote their interests. In this case the impact of bureaucratic politics will vary, reflecting political rivalries, the political climate and the shifting balance of power within government.[33] In light of the varying impact of bureaucratic politics, treating this analytical category as an independent variable would seem very problematic. Instead, the BPM should be exploited more modestly to provide a conceptual lens to examine the intra-governmental level. From this perspective, although the BPM will not develop into a normal science, the model's relevance for empirical research will likely endure. In particular, the BPM would seem useful to elucidate the constraints imposed by intra-governmental dynamics on rational foreign policy making including: intra-governmental communication failures; the difficulty faced by modern leaders in trying to control and monitor the bureaucratic apparatus; the constraints promoted by how organizations process and store information.

Rosenthal and 't Hart reinforce Welch's argument that the strength of the BPM lies not in its development as a scientific model, but rather in the conceptual and analytical framework it provides for empirical research on the impact of bureaucratic politics on foreign policy. They argue also that bureaucratic politics should adhere to a 'restrained BPM, defining bureaucratic politics as competitive and conflictual interaction between public agencies (or parts thereof) within the executive branch of government'. The authors challenge the claim made by some scholars, such as Freedman, that the scope of the BPM should be broadened to cover how bureaucratic politics play out in government as a whole. Rosenthal and 't Hart argue that this would reduce the explanatory purchase of the BPM. This reduction is evident in relation to a number of issues where, were the whole of government to be the unit of analysis, the BPM would not be adequate. For instance, it could not account for the relationships between politicians and bureaucratic elites and the nature and limits of bureaucratic power.[34]

So far we have explored the attempts of authors working within the positivist framework to rework the BPM. Another approach to revisit BPM is employing a critical constructivist approach, such as that of Weldes who seeks to reformulate the key concepts underpinning the model. This reformulation is based on three critical constructivist analytical commitments: '1) what we understand as "reality" is socially constructed and hence contestable, 2) constructions of reality both enact and reify relations of power, 3) an expressly critical constructivism requires that dominant constructions be denaturalized'.[35] Informed by these assumptions Weldes reworks three of the BPM's pivotal concepts: interests, power and rationality. Allison's positivist conception of the BPM noted earlier is challenged by bureaucratic interests not being perceived in material terms, for example, national security interests, organizational interests, domestic interests and personal interests. Rather, bureaucratic interests are deemed to be socially constructed, meaning that they are 'produced, reproduced, and transformed through the discursive practices of actors'.[36]

Correspondingly, interests do not flow from the material 'reality' defining a given situation. Rather, they emerge out of the *representations* that for actors define the situations and events they face. These representations are significant in so far as they form the basis for the social world of bureaucratic politics. In contrast to the positivist approaches of Allison and his followers, critical constructivists see the social world *not* merely as a realm for strategically pursuing predetermined bureaucratic interests, but as *constitutive* of interests. Correspondingly, a critical constructivist approach is concerned not only with uncovering what interests bureaucracies pursue but, more importantly, with the discursive and representational practices that render these interests valuable in the first place.

Power is another key concept that critical constructivists seek to 'denaturalize'. Power is central to the BPM because the model is based on the assumption that politics is a 'marketplace', involving pushing and hauling. In discussing the literature on BPM we note that power is understood in terms of the material resources with which individuals and bureaucracies equip themselves, to engage with each other in decision making and implementation, for example, bureaucratic position, money, information, prestige. For critical constructivists, however, power does not derive from these material resources, but lies in the discourse and representational practices of policy making. These discursive-representational practices are significant in determining 'who counts as an expert on a particular policy problem and so whose input, including that of various bureaucracies and individual bureaucratic actors, are heard and valued'.[37] For example, in a policy environment defined by a militaristic discourse, the army will be privileged over, say, the foreign ministry in determining how a state manages its foreign affairs, even though the foreign ministry might have the greater professional expertise in this area.[38] Thus, for critical constructivists reconceptualizing the notion of power in BPM is important for investigating empirically how institutional and discursive practices ultimately privilege some actors over others.

The emphasis placed by critical constructivists on discourse promotes critiques of the notion of rationality in relation to the BPM. Although Allison and his followers aimed to present the three models – rational, organizational and bureaucratic – as distinct, they all exhibit what Keohane terms a rationalist approach to decision making.[39] Through this prism rationality involves taking a decision relative to a *given* situation in order to 'maximize' or 'satisfice' goals.[40] Critical constructivists, however, reject the assumption that the importance of rationality lies in its representation of the choices that actors make and situations offer. Instead, we should recognize that at any given moment actors can choose among *multiple reasons*. Reasoning entails the production of meaning not merely through individual action, but through intersubjective *interaction*. From this vantage point the significance of actors' behaviour is expressed not by their choices, but by their depictions, which define the particular representations of the social world, its interests and policy problems. Choices, critical constructivists argue, flow from these representations because they *give* meaning to the particular situation at hand. Stemming from this reworking of the notion of rationality is a number of analytical tasks. One involves identifying characteristic modes of discourse and representation and explaining why some persist across disparate situations and events. Another analytical undertaking is to ascertain how particular modes of discourse and representation, institutions and individuals, are mutually reinforcing whilst others are marginalized. In this way, a critical constructivist approach depicts the discursive and representational conditions that shape choice, rather than analysis of the individual choice that is offered by the positivist approach to the BPM.

Conclusion

This chapter set out to examine the vibrant debate on BPM and explore the implications for foreign policy. Allison's work and that of his followers is crucial in terms of its recognition of the important role of bureaucracies in shaping foreign policy making and implementation. The thought-provoking assumptions in their early work prompted equally rich critiques. Allison's BPM was criticized for overstating the impact of bureaucracy over human agency. It was criticized for not being sufficiently analytically accurate about how and under what circumstances the impact of the bureaucracy prevails over other elements in government. The methodology of the BPM has been questioned too, especially with reference to the politics/logic dichotomy, the use of the game metaphor and the omission of non-bureaucratic foreign policy determinants. Questions have been raised about the feasibility of applying theories of the *firm* to the BPM. It is clear that some of these critiques have been addressed. For example, Hollis and Smith's notion of the role of foreign policy provides a more nuanced portrayal of the relationship between human agency and the bureaucratic imperative. Specifically, in showing that foreign policy roles are not static, are inconsistent and possess a relative autonomy from the bureaucracy, Hollis and Smith theoretically account for the leeway allowed to politicians to employ human agency within a bureaucratic structure. Similarly, Bendor and Hammond's work reinforces the claim that there is room for human agency within bureaucracy, by exposing the factors determining how and to what extent the head of the executive is obliged to bargain.

At the same time, the debate on BPM can be challenged, for example, in relation to its explanatory purchase compared to realism. We have explored the argument that, with the benefit of hindsight, Allison's rational policy model appears too simplistic. Indeed, before BPM can be seen as a real alternative to realism it must be seen to propose a more sophisticated rational policy model than that put forward by Allison. Bendor and Hammond's work is a good first step but more needs to be done. Another unresolved issue is whether the BPM could develop into normal science. Given the limitations highlighted by Welch's work, we would argue that it is unlikely that the BPM can confound the realists on their own positivist home ground. A much more productive route would be for BPM to adhere more closely to the general orientation of FPA, namely, by providing middle-range theories for empirical research. In this vein we believe that the BPM should be writ large, that is, that the unit of analysis should be the whole government rather than the executive. Understanding the impact of bureaucracies would seem impossible without their being placed in the context of the state in which they operate. We return to this issue in Chapter 5. Finally, radical constructivism opens new avenues for the BPM. Weldes's proposal to uncover how discursive and representational practices privilege certain interests and sources of power is an interesting avenue to pursue. Coupled with his idea about using the same technique to unveil how rationalities are constructed reveals the possible intersections between BPM and constructivism and also that constructivism and FPA more generally have the potential to cross-fertilize each other.

4   The domestic sources of foreign policy

Introduction

The adage 'politics stops at the water's edge' captures the tradition of foreign policy being an area where domestic political factionalism is sublimated to the interests of national security. This realist perspective on foreign policy and the communitarian pull of nationalism obscures both the complexity of decision making and the centrality of domestic factors in shaping the aims and outcomes of that process. Time-honoured questions such as who makes foreign policy and in whose interests, highlight the difficulty of ascribing simplistic, realist-tinged interpretations of foreign policy.

The problems inherent in defining what constitutes the 'national interest' inspired closer examination of the sources of foreign policy decision making and the nature of the process itself and extensive investigation of the individual decision maker and the role of bureaucratic influences in the formulation and implementation of foreign policy. This work, in turn, raises questions about how those elements outside the formal state structures of foreign policy decision making, but still within the sovereign confines of the state – societal actors, interests and values that reside in the domestic setting – are actually accounted for and integrated into the foreign policy process.

Domestic influences outside the formal state structures – lobbyists, the media, class factors, constitutional restrictions – are clearly significant and in some cases central to the making of state foreign policy.[1] For instance, societal actors, such as interest groups, actively engage the relevant state political actors in order to influence the foreign policy process in line with their concerns. At the same time, the formal and informal rules of political conduct within a given state are critical for shaping the manner in which this influence is exercised and the degree to which it is effective. Also, the overarching societal structure and its relationship to the state, that is, the role of elites and even class factors, can play a determining part in the orientation, access and particular forms that foreign policy assumes.

Reflecting this complex mosaic, within FPA there are three basic approaches to understanding the impact of domestic factors on state foreign policy. Each is rooted in a different account of state–society relations and, therefore, reflects the assumptions and interests of that particular depiction of those relations. One approach sees the principal source of domestic influence in the actual structural form (i.e. institutions and regimes) of the state. A second approach sees foreign policy making as being driven by the nature of the economic system within states and, concurrently, in the interests of a narrow elite that traditionally has acted in what it perceives to be the national interest. A third approach sees foreign policy as the product of a competitive pluralist environment as expressed by the interplay between interest group politics and state decision makers and structures. In Chapter 4, we focus on the enduring importance of the domestic setting in shaping foreign policy. In particular, we analyse the three accounts referred to above and examine efforts to model foreign policy decision making at the domestic level. Finally, the neglected role of political parties in foreign policy making process is discussed.

The enduring salience of the domestic

An understanding of the relationship between foreign policy, the state and the domestic environment necessarily requires an investigation of the nature of the state and society as a prerequisite to a discussion of how these actors can affect the foreign policy process. Concurrently, there needs to be some recognition that what constitutes the domestic environment and its array of actors and interests, is to a large extent an artifice which can be permeated by 'outside' forces.

While elsewhere in the book we discuss the role of the state – and its notable absence from the FPA literature – it is in scholarly work on the domestic environment that we find a more explicit commitment to established theoretical positions that reflect upon the nature of the state and its relationship to society. What these various approaches in FPA have in common is a belief that foreign policy is something that is produced and legitimized by the state apparatus, even if its sources reside within the domestic sphere. Based on this, domestic actors actively seek to capture the policy debate on foreign policy through a variety of means – from the dispensing of financial largesse to political mobilization strategies – and orient the policy choices made by the state towards their particular interests. Even those structuralist accounts which resist ascribing any autonomy of the state from societal – and in particular class interests – concede that factionalism within elite groups produces competition over foreign policy. Exactly how this process is said to occur is part of what differentiates the various approaches to the state.

Moreover what we are characterizing as the 'domestic environment' is itself an object of contestation. It is arguable that societies, even within recent memory, mirrored the relative isolation which accompanies subjection to the spatial confines of sovereign territorial boundaries to a greater degree than do contemporary societies. There were also temporal barriers between communities, a product of the slow methods of transport and communication over geographic distances throughout most of human history. These circumstances re-enforced the particularist character of different societies giving rise to notions of cultural specificity and associated practices. These beliefs have gained currency with the rising tide of globalization and inform much of the discourse on topics such as state decline, the homogenization of culture and the rise of global civil society (see Chapter 6 on globalization for more detail).[2]

At the same time, however, the historical record demonstrates that powerful ideas moved frequently in conjunction, for example, with the growing pace of international trade in earlier epochs such as in Europe in the sixteenth century. For instance, the reformist tracts that paved the way to Protestantism enjoyed a surprisingly robust circulation between city states and the patchwork of duchies, principalities and kingdoms that formed Europe's regional political system at that time. More recently, the phenomenal absorption of cellular phone technology by African societies – the world's poorest, saddled with abysmal infrastructures and as a result among the most isolated societies in the world – demonstrates that these seemingly adverse conditions need not be an insurmountable barrier. Perhaps it is a failure on our part, giddy from the near instantaneous forms of global communication, to imagine and recognize the possibilities inherent in slower forms of information sharing, and the hunger for knowledge and communication among peoples separated only by geography.

This bundling of domestic and international concerns, captured by the unfortunate term 'inter-mestic', tends to make foreign policy issues subject to influence both external and internal to the territorial state to varying degrees. As far back as the 1970s, Peter Gourevitch recognized the possibilities of external influence over the shape and tenor of domestic debates – especially but not exclusively in relation to foreign policy issues.[3] He suggested that Waltz's 'second image', that is, the state level of analysis, is the 'reverse' of the conventional depiction in which influence flows only outward, from the domestic setting to the external environment. Mansbach, Ferguson and Lampert use the analogy of a cobweb to describe the international system and to capture the structural implications of this insight, depicting a process of constant interaction between state and non-state actors.[4] In the face of ideas and pressures from abroad permeating state borders coupled with an ever-expanding web of international norms, rules and regimes designed to regulate state conduct in particular spheres, the capacity of foreign policy decision makers to construct their policy formulations and actions with sole reference to domestic forces, seems ever more remote.

Nevertheless, despite the prevailing rapid circulation of ideas, pressures and material goods characteristic of the contemporary global setting, there are some defining features of the international political system that allow for reference to the enduring saliency and indeed centrality of the domestic environment in the foreign policy process. Fundamental among these is the legal status accorded to the idea of sovereignty, which, of course, gives to the state primacy over a fixed territory and its population. Recognition of the rights of governments within states to exercise this authority even with the emergence of a discourse on the 'responsibility to protect', and the inability of societies to have alternative means of expressing their political aspirations other than through sovereignty, is a powerful, defining characteristic of the international system. The fact of citizenship is an acknowledgement of the constraints on individual action. Moreover, the legal structures of states, which provide formal status to corporative entities ranging from businesses to NGOs, define the parameters to their conduct.[5] The establishment of tax havens in island states, the movement of multinationals from one state to another in search of the most beneficial tax and labour conditions, and the utilization of territory to accommodate political refugees are all signs that states and the domestic conditions within them are crucial sites of relatively autonomous political (and economic) activity, which should be considered with the utmost seriousness. This is given concrete expression through everything from corporate taxes, the possibility of lawsuits and the degree of media freedom that is specific to the particular domestic setting of a given state.

Socio-cultural influences – reflected for example by governing practices in different states – introduce local variation into what otherwise might be relative homogeneity within regions.[6] The adoption of western ideas of sovereignty, for instance, has not been wholesale, but rather has been a process mediated by local elites and aligned to their needs, established institutions and foundational ideas. This process – which Amitav Acharya characterizes as 'norm localization' – gives primacy to domestic actors, institutions and settings in assessing the salience of 'foreign' ideas in relation to prevailing local circumstances.[7] This reassertion of the domestic in the trajectory of the norm cycle is not only a cogent explanation for the partial adaptation or even rejection of externally sourced ideas, for example, in relation to women's rights by 'non-western' societies, but also reminds us that local societal factors exercise a determining influence over ideational matters.[8]

Finally, the indisputable position of the foreign policy decision makers within this complex setting at the centre of a sovereign-based system of authority, derives its substantive legitimacy from the domestic society, which is reified in legal terms by the international system. While these policy decision makers may seek sometimes to boost their standing and prestige by appealing to international actors, ultimately and crucially their authority is dependent upon domestic sources.

The domestic structures approach: constitutional structures and political regimes

For many FPA scholars, the most significant source of foreign policy is the domestic structure of the nature of the state political institutions, the features of society and the institutional arrangements linking state and society and channelling societal demands into the political system. Katzenstein, Krasner, Risse-Kappen and others provide detailed descriptions of the relative strengths and weakness governing relations between differing state structures and society.[9]

According to Risse-Kappen, for instance, the importance of the state structure resides in the fact that it is the crucial site of foreign policy decision making and, mediated through constitutional arrangements, is the area where state and society 'negotiate' the country's international relations.[10] Here, within the particular constitutional framework of the state, domestic institutions and interest groups operate, devising coalition-building strategies that ultimately demonstrate the effectiveness of domestic influences over foreign policy. The rules of political participation influence formal politics and the conduct of political parties in relation to international issues. Traditionally, the executive has the authority to formulate and implement foreign policy, endowed by the constitution or convention; the legislature and other institutions have limited powers of judicial review and budgetary control.

The number of points of access between societal groups and decision makers determines the degree to which there is public input to state foreign policy. For example, France has very few access points to the executive and is 'state-dominated' because the public plays only a limited role in foreign policy making; in the US there are multiple access points to the executive, foreign policy is 'society-dominated' and the public has many opportunities to influence it.[11]

Another aspect of the domestic structure that influences foreign policy is the political regime type. Authoritarian regimes with no electoral mandate from their populations and historically have used foreign issues to distract from domestic difficulties. George Kennan's 'X telegram' and subsequent articulation of America's 'containment policy' towards the Soviet Union was predicated on just such an analysis of the roots of Soviet foreign policy.[12] From this perspective, democratic (or 'pluralist') regimes tend to pursue fewer foreign policy 'adventures' that are out of step with the interests of their society. However, research shows that lack of access to information and other bureaucratic obstacles constructed by authoritarian states may also exist in democratic states and restrict public involvement in foreign policy decision making.[13] The differences between these two types of regimes in this respect are sometimes small.

In the context of regime-oriented considerations of the domestic origins of foreign policy there is the 'democratic peace debate', which derives from Kant's 'perpetual peace' theory and his model of an international order which only 'republican' states are allowed to join. Michael Doyle replacing the term 'republican' with 'liberal', points to statistical analyses that support the fact that stable constitutional liberal democracies do not engage in wars with one another.[14] His rationale is, first, that a 'cultural-normative' interpretation suggests that stable democracies resolve conflict through negotiation and bargaining and, therefore, favour these same approaches in foreign policy, especially towards other democratic regimes. However, in the context of non-democratic regimes, democratic leaders cast off their inhibitions in relation to conflict. Concurrently, a 'structural-institutional' interpretation suggests that democratic regimes are founded on a system of checks and balances that effectively slow decision making while emphasizing the public agreement with foreign policy decisions in relation to the declaration of war, all of which serves as an internal deterrent to promulgating war between democracies. Although the empirical basis for democratic peace theory is open to contestation on several grounds, there is general acceptance that the data broadly supports this proposition.[15]

The notion of 'middle powers' introduces another variant into the relationship between political regime and foreign policy behaviour. Cooper, Higgot and Nossal propose that ideational and material attributes combine to contribute to a self-conscious assertion of national role – echoing some of the work on role theory – that produces distinctive foreign policy conduct in high-income but 'middle ranked states such as Canada and Australia'.[16] Middle power foreign policies are usually multilateralist, bridge-building and concerned with the promotion of norms. Some scholars include developing countries, such as Malaysia and South Africa, in the group of middle power states.[17] This approach to identifying middle powers is rooted in the prevailing power hierarchies of states (and avoids trying to develop objective material indicators for their rankings), and relies on domestic perceptions of capacity in relation both to other states and to the particular sector (such as trade) or foreign policy issue under consideration.

Scholarship on political regimes within different geographic regions has moved away from analyses of the impact of regimes on foreign policy, to emphasize the regional systemic patterns and local particulars of history and society in shaping foreign policy conduct. For instance, Africanists studying foreign policy who seek to integrate their work into the established typologies of African political regimes, for example, neo-patrimonial to settler oligarchies believe that these have exercised a determining influence over the structures of foreign policy decision making and implementation.[18] In studies of the foreign policy of Middle Eastern states the predominance of authoritarian states backed by security services has been noted.[19] In Southeast Asia, the convergence of elite interests and cultural specificities has produced a regional foreign policy style which some academics and practitioners characterize as the 'ASEAN (Association of South East Asian Nations) way'.[20]

In some ways, this trend echoes earlier thinking in FPA related to the diagnosis of 'nation-type' and national attribute theory as a means of developing a comprehensive predictive analysis of foreign policy behaviour.[21] However, unlike the comparative FPA project, there as yet is no renewal of the effort to systematize these particularist features into a rigorously drawn and universal rationalist framework (much less one that seeks to codify the variables as in the comparative FPA project).[22] Stephen Krasner, while critical of what he characterizes as structural approaches to the analysis of state foreign policies, proposes an approach that takes the historical evolution of the state as a starting point for understanding foreign policy conduct.[23] Work on regions, such as Buzan and Weaver's regional security complexes, seems to be anticipating a return to the systematic consideration of foreign policy conduct through its emphasis on the specificities of local factors as a way of interpreting regional state behaviour. Laura Neack's attempt to link state type to foreign policy conduct, which includes a focus on the category of 'middle powers', is an example of such an approach.[24]

The 'structuralist' approach: economic systems and social class

Among structuralist writings in the Marxist tradition, we can find the roots of foreign policy and, more particularly, the motivation for exploitative policies, such as imperialism and colonialism, in the nature of the capitalist economic system. According to Karl Marx, although the state may be nothing more than a committee representing bourgeois interests, it performs a critical function in ordering the interests of capital in relation to labour and markets.[25] This instrumentalist view denies the existence of state autonomy in real terms, but suggests that state legitimacy is dependent on the population having a perception of its autonomy.[26] The literature is dominated by debates on the relative autonomy of the state from the elites, but those scholars in this tradition agree that a narrow social class uses its control over the economy to ensure that foreign policy conforms to its interests.

For structuralists, the crucial divisions between the hierarchy of the states fitted within the international political economy are the most important guide to foreign policy conduct. A centre–periphery relationship, based upon the economic exploitation of non- and semi-industrialized states of the 'Third World' (or the south), produces a foreign policy oriented towards maintaining this relationship between the industrialized core and the countries of the periphery. Bruce Moon examines how the 'peripheral state' is driven by the need for domestic legitimacy – bolstered by international recognition – alongside the pursuit of economic or developmental aims.[27] Capturing the state is crucial for domestic actors to enhance their accumulation of resources. Robert Cox and Hein Marais, among others, suggest that in the developing countries there is a transnational capitalist class, which shares the norms and values of the leading capitalist countries, fostered by leading international institutions such as the World Bank.[28] These local elites actively subvert local considerations in favour of their capitalist interests and, in so doing, perpetuate the exploitative relations of economic dominance. This explains the foreign policy orientation towards western interests, in matters such as trade liberalization, by otherwise impoverished states, whose domestic industries and agricultural sector suffer from open market access.

Finally, there is a strand in the literature on class and elite foreign policy theory that describes foreign policy as conducted by and for the elite within society. Skidmore and Hudson characterize this approach as the 'social bloc' model, in which power is concentrated in the hands of a social minority which produces a drive for a more cohesive elite and a relatively stable domestic environment. As a result, political leaders can emerge only through alliance to one of a few dominant social blocs whose well-articulated interests are reflected in the foreign policy implemented.[29] The breakdown of this cohesion, for example, in the case of the Philippines under the Marcos regime and Nigeria under General Suni Abacha, can provoke political crisis that can lead to the broadening of political participation in an effort to re-legitimize the political system. Christopher Clapham holds that the overarching imperative of state survival compels African elites to use foreign policy as an instrument to obtain economic resources and political legitimacy from the external environment.[30]

The relationship between the institutions of foreign policy making and the interests of the dominant economic and social forces in society has been studied in depth. The nineteenth-century English observer, John Bright, noted that the members of the diplomatic corps essentially were drawn from the elite and he suggested that 'foreign policy is a gigantic system of outdoor relief for the aristocracy'.[31] In the mid-twentieth century, the American political scientist Charles Wright Mills identified a 'power elite', composed of corporate leaders, politicians and military commanders, as the driving force behind foreign (and national) policy.[32] The ability of these groups to construe parochial concerns as 'national interest' and, thus, dictate foreign policy, is tied to their capacity to maintain an overarching social cohesion that allows them to continue to mobilize society through ideological and economic appeals.

The pluralist approach: sub-state societal actors and interests

Pluralism is perhaps the most widely acknowledged approach to assessing the role and impact of domestic factors on foreign policy. Pluralism includes the myriad of sub-state and non-state actors within the domestic arena and their efforts to exert influence over state institutions and decision-making processes. In this depiction of the state, its autonomy is assumed (as in the classic Weberian approach), but implies also a more explicitly atomized and competitive depiction of state–society relations. The general preponderance of domestic over international concerns, from this perspective, is a function of the variety of societal interest groups and the cross-cutting cleavages among them.[33] Because foreign policy issues affect the material interests of different societal groups differently, these groups compete and mobilize for influence over political decision making. The focus in the pluralist approach is primarily on electoral democracies and the role of sub-state and non-state actors, principally interest groups, public opinion and the media, in shaping the foreign policy choices of decision makers.

Interest groups are distinguished by their sources of support and the nature of their interests. They offer either political mobilization for electoral support or financial mobilization for electoral support (or both), to governments and political parties, in exchange for their backing for foreign policy positions. A key variable in this exchange is the degree to which interest groups are able to mobilize and present their positions, at least in ideological terms, as responsive to collective (or national) concerns. The number of techniques used to achieve these aims has grown in line with new telecommunications/communication technologies and the growth of new media. Interest groups can be categorized roughly as lobby groups, single-issue movements, constituency-based groups (e.g. ethnic minority voters) and special interest groups (e.g. representatives of a particular industry).[34] Research into interest groups' influence on foreign policy focuses mainly on the economic and political aspects, for example, the impact of particular business lobbies on a state's commercial policies or the role of ethnic lobbies in promoting their respective concerns. Security issues, from this perspective, are a matter of national interest and, therefore, domestic factionalism is set aside. David Skidmore challenges this view, demonstrating that the rise of foreign and security lobbies, ranging from defence industry groups to non-governmental 'peace' organizations, such as the American Friends Committee (Quakers), are a clear indicative that society does hold distinctive and sometimes deeply contradictory views on security matters.[35]

Public opinion is a broad term that encompasses the mass, attentive public and various interest groups and lobby groups. Public opinion sets the parameters to foreign policy decisions and can be seen as a 'background' restraint on foreign policy making and implementation. The concept of public opinion is problematic since it requires definition of who is the public and involves debate on the methodologies adopted to promote the public's viewpoints. Christopher Hill, in his study of British public opinion on foreign policy, characterizes public opinion as 'the Loch Ness monster', something frequently spoken about, but never seen.[36]

The classical Almond–Lippman view holds that public opinion should have no role or influence over foreign policy and it is largely indifferent to and ignorant of foreign policy issues. Subscribers to this consensus believe that the public's attitudes are mercurial and inconsistent and therefore a poor – and even dangerous – source of foreign policy making. For these reasons, they argue persuasively for a governing elite to manage foreign policy.[37] Shapiro and Page disagree, demonstrating in their study of US foreign policy during the CW, that public opinion was not only consistent – as shown by numerous studies of democracies – but quite 'rational' in its assessment of international events.[38] James Rosenau studies public opinion based on a pyramid where the peak is the elite (the government, the legislature and the media); the second level is the attentive public (intellectuals and business); and the third level is the general public (who are indifferent).[39] Several scholars suggest that only a section of public opinion, perhaps between 5 and 20 per cent, is interested in and attentive to foreign policy. Public interest seems to depend upon the issue (also known as 'issue saliency'). Routine issues related to diplomacy are not high on the agenda of public concerns, but economic and trade issues and questions related to war and peace arouse the public interest.[40]

It is clear that a discussion of public opinion without a concomitant theory of the media will be incomplete. The *media* play a crucial, if controversial, role in the foreign policy process, in acting as a bridge for the passage of information between the public, the state and the international arena. The media's influence on foreign policy can be considered in our view from three perspectives: agenda setting, information clearing house and government propaganda tool. The media as an agenda setter is exemplified in the role of William Randolph Hearst, an American newspaper mogul, whose bellicose editorials and reportage promoted American military action in the late nineteenth century. A contemporary example is the so-called 'CNN effect', or the degree to which media spotlight on a particular issue forces the state to take action.[41] Research into government responses to portrayals of humanitarian crises indicates that while the media can play an important role in shaping foreign policy at the height of a crisis, its influence wanes as the crisis – or coverage of it – declines.

The media as a 'clearing house' is predicated upon an implicit sense of its institutional neutrality. Editorial policy is not as much a function of ideological perspectives, established interests or personal biases, but rather an ordering of information that conforms to the wants and needs of the citizenry. Market factors and consumer conduct, therefore, are the main drivers of media action and impose a logic on the particular sector that defies efforts to give it overt direction. The fact that disaster and sex promote sales of newspapers and other media, means that these sorts of stories will be prioritized in order to increase circulation.

The media as a government propaganda tool certainly holds for closed, authoritarian states that seek to manage the flow of information to their citizens in the interests of regime security. The more controversial position is that democratic polities deliberately engage in manipulating the public in order to steer foreign policy in directions that suit elite interests. Noam Chomsky characterizes the process of opinion formation in democracies as 'manufactured consent', in which the state and the media elites shape citizens' outlooks to conform to their particular interests in order to gain support for the pursuit of a specific foreign policy agenda.[42] Following this insight, several studies suggest that it is only when elite opinion within a state is divided over foreign policy that the media can exert influence over public opinion. For example, the UK media and the public outcry against the Blair government's participation in the last Iraq war reflected divisions within the foreign policy establishment over this policy.

Having an input into the media is a priority for democratic states seeking the approval of the public for a particular course of action. Following the Vietnam War, the US government tried to influence the media, which was seen as being an independent actor capable of undermining the government's foreign policy objectives. The influence exerted included the introduction of new approaches to managing media (daily briefings, controlled leaks, spin and 'embedded journalists'). State-funded media, such as the UK British Broadcasting Corporation (BBC), present a somewhat different set of problems for a democratic state since they raise the issue of a balance between independence and control of the media agenda. Another source of information on international affairs is non-state actors whose mandate is to shape public opinion on foreign policy issues. These include 'think tanks', such as the numerous (nearly 300 in 2011) strategic studies centres across the world, philanthropic foundations, such as the Carnegie Endowment for International Peace, and semi-state actors such as political party foundations, for example, Germany's Friedrich Ebert Foundation and the US National Endowment for Democracy.[43] MNCs use their funding of non-state actors to support perspectives that correspond with their interests. Advocacy groups, such as environmentalists or human rights activists, try to mobilize public support (and in so doing influence government action) through media campaigns designed to raise awareness of their issues and concerns.

Finally, new media, especially computer-enabled media, have provided non-state actors and individuals with numerous platforms, such as 'blog' sites and social networks, to connect people and provide information. There is a dizzying array of alternative narratives and stories, sometimes available in 'real time', which make it very difficult for governments to keep abreast of events and enables the 'spinning' of public opinion. The extraordinary efforts exerted by authoritarian states to control the Internet (e.g. in Cuba, Iran and China) are testament to the fear that these instruments induce, and the outbreak of revolution in North Africa in 2011 served to confirm this fear. The longer-term implications for governance that accompany the fragmentation of national media into narrower interest-based constituencies that are market or interest driven, and the implications for opinion formation on foreign policy have yet to be thoroughly explored.

Modelling foreign policy decision making in the domestic environment

The inherent complexity involved in interpreting foreign policy formulation and choice has inspired different approaches to modelling this process. These approaches mirror the classic three levels of analysis in FPA focusing on the role of the individual leader, the place of state institutions and the influence of system factors, in their assessment of foreign policy decision making in the domestic environment. Joe Hagan and Julia Kaarbo having written about the competitive role played by political actors within government structures in their efforts to understand the dynamics of foreign policy choice; Robert Putnam, Robert Keohane and Joseph Nye have developed approaches to foreign policy which seek to account for the complexity and interplay between the domestic and external forces.

Hagan revisits the role of leaders in democratic governments as the focal points of foreign policy decision making.[44] He holds that a leader's primary concern is political survival in office, and that all policy choices ultimately are set against the backdrop of this *sine qua non*. The task of the leader becomes one of creating and maintaining coalitions of support for the respective foreign policy agendas through a central concern over ways of managing opposition to that agenda from within the governing party or from the formal opposition party. Hagan posits that this is achieved through the application of one of three strategies, accommodation, insulation or mobilization. In the case of accommodation, the leader bargains with the opponents to the foreign policy agenda to win support for a compromise foreign policy.

Insulation involves deflecting attention away from the foreign policy issue in question thus freeing the 'political space' for the leader's preferred foreign policy action. A mobilization strategy is pursued to win support for a foreign policy position by persuading opponents of the policy.

Kaarbo delves into the actual governing structures and examines the role of bureaucracies – especially of minority dissenters to the prevailing policy choices – in the foreign policy process. According to Kaarbo, the ability of these bureaucratic minorities to influence foreign policy is based on their familiarity with and consequent facility at manipulating the decision-making procedures and information within governing structures.[45] Their minority standing, due to the fact that they are directly subordinate within a particular bureaucratic institution (a vertical minority) or because they are part of a weaker bureaucratic institution among more prominent bureaucratic institutions (a horizontal minority), helps to determine the specific strategic approach adopted to promote their position.

Pluralist studies of foreign policy recognize the impact of a diversity of actors, salient international institutions and a changing environment on foreign policy decision making. This growing complexity poses significant challenges to the more conventional explanations of foreign policy conduct in FPA. In attempting to address this, Martin Rochester identifies four problems facing foreign policy makers engaged in classic pursuits of national interest in the context of the pluralist 'cobweb' paradigm: satisfying different interest groups affected unequally by foreign policy; sub-national actors with cross-cutting affiliations and interests; controlling the conduct of MNCs with their own specific interests; and satisfying both the domestic and a foreign constituencies.[46]

In Chapter 2 we discussed how Robert Putnam responded to this last challenge by devising an approach based on the two-level game which reflects the two environments of decision making.[47] Putnam's approach to modelling foreign policy decision making – which focuses on trade issues, but was seen by FPA scholars as having wider applicability – aims to integrate and understand the different (and sometimes rival) dynamics involved in a given foreign policy choice. According to Putnam, decision makers have to operate within two competing frameworks with different rules and different operational logics – the external environment which is anarchic, and the domestic environment which operates under recognized rules – in order to achieve a 'win-set' (a policy that satisfies all requisite interests). The weighing of options, the classic 'guns versus butter' problem (security versus wealth creation) in the decision on a specific foreign policy matter is made more complex by the different sets of rules governing these two environments. Putnam's influential approach is informed by game theory and captures the dynamic attempts of decision makers to address local constituencies and external forces simultaneously.

Finally, Keohane and Nye proposed a model of foreign policy decision making which echoes the very complexity it seeks to explain. 'Complex inter-dependency' allows the state to retain a measure of agency in assessing and mobilizing state and sub-state actors, NGOs and international institutions for its own ends.[48] The increasing relevance of international institutions is reflected in the fact that international institutions are seen as the prime arena for action (though implicitly the UN is recognized as an autonomous international actor). Keohane and Nye's portrayal of the foreign policy process as interlinked through a variety of networks, actors and interests anticipates key features of the globalization literature, although unlike Held and others, they hold fast to neo-realist assumptions about the centrality of the state, the continuing relevance of the domestic environment and its role in defining motivations for action.

Political parties – the neglected element

These approaches to framing and interpreting foreign policy decision making within the domestic context provide some insights into this complex process. At the same time, with the exception of Hagan, they mostly neglect the part played by political parties in this process. In many respects, political parties can be seen as the key site for a number of activities attributed in FPA to domestic sources of foreign policy. These include the simultaneous role of political parties as agenda setters in foreign policy, through ideological discourses reflecting their distinctive political orientation (e.g. rightist or leftist), as agenda followers in foreign policy, and through their position as interest aggregators derived from the support they court from within domestic society.

Closer examination of political parties and foreign policy reveals that many of the determining points in the formulation of ideological orientation and particular policy choices (which sometimes appear directly contradictory to this orientation) of a state's foreign policy are products of the decisions and inputs at the political party level, and not formal government. Moreover, by focusing on political parties and foreign policy it is possible to move away from the normative tendency towards concentrating on democratic forms of governance and imbuing them with special attributes to examining dispassionately how single-party regimes, for example, the Communist Party of China, operate in ways that mimic these key functions. Political parties utilize their international networks in ways that complement, supplement or even contradict the formal diplomatic bilateral state apparatus. During the CW, for example, the West German political parties and their foundations maintained links that cut across the diplomatic necessity to recognize East Germany.[49] The international departments of socialist, social democratic, liberal and communist parties all, to varying degrees, exercise a form of 'foreign policy', which is at once deeply ideological, highly political and resoundingly statist in its underlying ambitions. Although a lack of party discipline and the power of lobbies have blunted the power of political parties in the US, it would be a mistake to ignore the important organizing functions they perform within the political system.

Marrying the insights from scholarship on domestic structure to how different political regimes configure political participation is a critical follow-up to the incorporation of political parties into foreign policy decision making. It would provide a richer account of the arena of political action and provide some clarity for our understanding of the dynamics of interest-based politics and their impact on foreign policy choice. The 'shadow politics' of influence peddling, often only dredged up in the wake of political scandal, could give new meaning to our understanding of the competitive world of pluralist politics.

Conclusion

The approaches discussed above – a domestic structures rendering, a classical structuralist account and the pluralist approach – are important elements in the 'conversation' on the significance, role and influence of the domestic environment in foreign policy. We explored the intersection between domestic influences and regional locations. The difficulty inherent in incorporating some of these insights regarding abstract notions, such as public opinion, into a working model of foreign policy decision making, somewhat limit their interpretive value.

However, through Hagan's portrayal of leadership in foreign policy and Putnam's 'two-level game', we can see how decision makers might manage the competing pressures and concerns in developing state foreign policy. We have shown that the domestic environment is a crucial and constraining factor in foreign policy and puts limits on what is possible in national foreign policy. Nonetheless, it is clear that contemporary foreign policy is not focused only on the externalization of domestic politics, but is part of a complex interchange across the domestic–foreign state frontier.

5 Foreign policy analysis and the state

Introduction

As already noted, for many years IR was dominated by the realist concept of the state, which perceives the state as a unitary, rational actor pursuing a supreme national interest (survival) within an anarchic international environment. Some have branded this notion 'national-territorial totality' since conceptually the state comprises the 'country as a whole and all that is within it: territory, government, people, and society'.[1] Throughout this book, different strands of FPA reject this realist conception. The literature on the impact of psychological factors challenges the rationality ascribed by realism to the state, and the notion of bureaucratic politics problematizes the perception of the state as a unitary actor. Research on the impact of domestic players and transnational actors (TNAs) also questions the insularity afforded by realists to the state and its foreign policy. Although foreign policy analysts' critiques underline the conceptual and analytical limitations of realism, FPA creates other problems: it unpacks the state to the point that the concept of the state disappears.

Arguably, this creates three tensions. Epistemologically, middle-range FPA theories, although lacking an explicit conceptualization of the state, draw on a range of tacit assumptions about what the state actually is. These drive the thinking of foreign policy analysts in ways that are not overtly recognizable. Ontologically, because the state is considered to be no more than an extension of the elements within middle-range theory it becomes difficult, if not impossible, to account for foreign policy as a distinct site of action. Finally, a significant conceptual and analytical tension within FPA arises because in studying the formulation and implementation of foreign policy, FPA recognizes that the state enjoys a degree of autonomy from the society it rules and external actors. However, since the concept of state is not explicit in

FPA, this autonomy cannot be discussed in either conceptual or analytical terms.

This chapter aims to resolve the aforementioned tensions by drawing on the rich debate between IR and historical sociology (HS). Since its launch in the mid-1980s, this debate has contributed to the development of several strands of IR theory,[2] although it has been overlooked by FPA.[3] In our view, this is a missed intellectual opportunity; since HS has advanced debate over the state in IR, it should be applied to the problem of the state in FPA. This would mean, first, conceptually and analytically reconciling FPA and conceptions of the state within HS and, second, exploring the implications of this analytical and conceptual reconciliation, for key notions in FPA. Third, it would enable a conceptual sketching of ideal-state types that would reflect the diversity of states in the contemporary international system. We propose three such ideal types: the institutional state, the quasi-state and the clustered state. These classifications, which do not fully capture all states in the contemporary international system, should be seen as a preliminary to further refinements of these concepts.

The institutional state

Prior to the mid-1980s IR was dominated by three competing theoretical conceptions of the state: realism, which emphasized the primacy of the state in determining IR; pluralism, which highlighted the roles of non-state actors through the notion of interdependence;[4] and global system theory, which saw state behaviour as derived from the exigencies imposed by socio-economic or politico-military structures.[5] By the mid-1980s, none of these approaches prevailed or had proved to be more incisive than the others.[6] This impasse in IR contrasted with a revival of debate on the state in sociology. A first wave of neo-Weberian historical sociology (WHS), represented by the work of Skocpol, Tilly and Giddens, developed an 'institutionalized conception' of the state.[7] The pertinence of this conception for IR was its contrast to the realist conception of the state. Instead of the state being conceived of in terms of a territorial totality, it was seen as 'a set of administrative, policing and military organisations headed, and more or less well coordinated, by an executive authority'.[8] In this formulation the state is an 'actual organisation' possessing relative autonomy and the capacity to act in the internal and external spheres. The relative autonomy of the state in either context derives from its unique positioning to deal with the exigencies imposed by international security competition, the ongoing need to extract finance, for example, via taxation, to fund its endeavours, and its capacity for surveillance. States use surveillance of civil society in order to both pacify it and mobilize its resources. The state–civil society relationship is one of competition in which the state has relative autonomy.[9]

The path-breaking work by Tilly, Skocpol and Giddens was followed by an equally impressive second wave of neo-WHS writings. Mann, perhaps more than any other of these scholars, produced work that most pertains to the debate on the state in IR.[10] Mann defines the state as '1) a differentiated set of institutions and personnel embodying centrality; 2) in the sense that political relations radiate to and from a centre to cover; 3) a territorially demarcated area, over which it exercises and; 4) some degree of authoritative, binding rule-making, backed up by some organised physical force'.[11]

Before examining the differences between the first and the second waves of neo-WHS writing, it is helpful to explore the common ground in neo-WHS conceptions of the state, and their implications for FPA. Mann, in line with the first wave of neo-WHS writing, sees the state as a separate institutional entity, simultaneously rooted in the domestic and external environments, with the capacity to act and with relative autonomy. The notion of the state's embeddedness in the internal and external spheres fits with the depiction in FPA of foreign policy as a boundary activity: an activity that occurs at the interface between the domestic and the external spheres. Also, portraying the state as an organization, and an organization that can act, implies that it plays a central part in determining foreign policy, but also is separate from other defining factors. In contrast to the state's portrayal in realism, it is at the centre of the analysis, but does not eclipse other foreign policy determinants.

Having examined the assumptions common to the first and second waves of neo-WHS conceptions of the state, we need to look at the propositions that distinguish them. This exercise is aimed at establishing how the second wave of WHS, embodied in Mann's work, advances our understanding of the institutional state and has helped to refine some key concepts of FPA. Mann in contrast to Tilly, Giddens and Skocpol, does not see the political relations between state and society in terms only of coercion/competition. Mann's definition emphasizes that political relations *radiate* from civil society to the state, and from the state outwards.[12] Accordingly, Mann distinguishes between two forms of power. *Despotic power*, which 'refers to the distributive power of state elites over civil society, and derives from the range of actions that state elites can undertake without routine negotiation with civil society groups'.[13] *Infrastructural power,* which is the 'institutional capacity of a central state, despotic or not, to penetrate its territories and logistically implement decisions'.[14] Infrastructural power, in contrast to despotic power, is a two-way street: it enables civil society parties to permeate the state.

The notion that political relations radiate to and from the state, and the corollary that states can possess despotic *and* infrastructural power, is significant for the FPA conceptualization of the relationship between state, society and foreign policy. We noted in Chapter 4 that societal FPA approaches perceive the state as pervaded by multiple actors operating in the domestic sphere.[15] Liberals, in their turn, see the state as embodying society's demands and values through formally institutionalized arrangements: constitutions, elections, legislative frameworks, etc. Marxists emphasize economic systems and class. Mann's work furnishes FPA with a fourth way to conceptualize state–society relations, hinging on the idea that the coercive and extractive nature of the state, and its surveillance capacity, affords it a relative autonomy from domestic societal forces. Thus, the state will only *partially* reflect the needs and values of its society. Similarly, the relative autonomy of the state imposes limits on the degree to which societal actors can make an impact. The task of FPA is to evaluate how the impact of societal actors and the effect of their values and demands affect foreign policy, but also broaden the canvas. FPA also needs to assess how foreign policy making and its implementation reflect *a balance* among promoting society's needs and values, being subject to pressure from societal actors, and possessing relative autonomy.

Mann's definition is distinguished also by its reference to the institutions *and* personnel comprising the state. This represents a departure from conventional Weberian wisdom that the modern state is differentiated institutionally from society. In Mann's account, the state does not merely follow a formal/instrumental rationality that is distinct from the substantive or value rationality found in the private sphere of civil society. Rather, social and personal influences, for example, identities, norms, psychological profiles, percolate through the state via the bureaucrats and statesmen and stateswomen in charge.[16] The notion that the impacts of individual factors affect the state provides a refinement to the work of FPA on the effect of psychological, cognitive, bureaucratic and identity factors. Within FPA the effect of these factors is examined in isolation from the institutional landscape of the state. For this reason, foreign policy accounts emerge as no more than the sum of the individual or bureaucratic parts. Through the prism of Mann's work, however, the impact of individual/bureaucratic foreign policy factors is set against the particular institutional landscape of the state.

In our view, this provides a more balanced, more analytically nuanced understanding of how individuals and bureaucracies, operating within the context of the state, affect foreign policy. As noted in Chapters 2 and 3, FPA largely ignores the distinctive state context in which decision making and bureaucratic politics take place.

Finally, in Mann's definition, the state exercises some degree of control (though not monopoly) over authoritative, binding rule making, backed by an organized physical force. On the assumption that there is no monopoly over the use of organized physical force, this suggests that the state relies on other sources of power to exercise its authority and make binding rules. Mann, therefore, examines the development of states through the ideology, economic, military, political (IEMP) model 'so called for its four central dimensions: ideological, economic, military and political power relations'.[17] In the IEMP model the state is not reduced to any single power source; rather, these sources of power are present simultaneously in society and have a mutually constitutive relationship with the state. The degree to which each power source dominates at any given time depends on the conditions underpinning the particular historical juncture.[18] This led Mann to develop his theory of the polymorphous state 'wherein the state crystallizes in multiple contexts – domestic or international, ideological, economic, military and political'.[19] His account perceives the state as 'messier' than in the first wave of WHS thinking, and much more so than realism would concede. It foregrounds the middle-range theoretical and methodological FPA approach within a conceptual framework that emphasizes the contingent and context-specific nature of foreign policy making and its implementation.

The quasi-state

Analytical reconciliation of the institutional debate and some key FPA concepts helps resolve some of the tensions identified earlier in this chapter. The institutional conception of the state is informed by a Weberian epistemology of the state, making clear the foreign policy analyst's assumptions about the state. In ontological terms the state is identified as a separate actor. Thus, the state's foreign policy is not reduced to the sum of its individual or bureaucratic parts. Neither is the state's foreign policy merely a product of the pressures imposed by external structures. In fact, we have shown that an institutional understanding of the state accounts, conceptually and analytically, for the state's relative autonomy. Since foreign policy is acknowledged to be a key activity of the state, then by inference, we can identify, in conceptual and analytical terms, the source of foreign policy autonomy. What is of interest, however, is whether all states conform to the institutional depiction of the state and, if not, what other types of state can we identify from the HS literature, and what are their implications for FPA?

This section explores these issues in the context of what Robert Jackson identifies as quasi-states.[20] The notion of quasi-states refers, in particular, to the states in the 'global south', represented by the colonial territories in Africa, Asia and the Pacific and the Caribbean. Like independent countries, quasi-states possess 'juridical statehood: legal recognition as sovereign states from international organizations and major powers'.[21] However, in many cases the institutions endowing territorial statehood, for example, the coercive apparatus, the political institutions, the money-extracting mechanisms, surveillance capacity, are fragmented and incomplete. While quasi-states may enjoy equal legal sovereignty, they lack the institutions able to constrain and outlast the individuals occupying their offices.[22] They can be described as partially accomplished states, or quasi-states. A corollary of partial institutional statehood is that the states affected depend, to a greater extent than the institutional concept of state would concede, on the rules, norms and institutions underpinning contemporary international society.[23] The contemporary society that emerged after World War II (WWII), and which began to replace the international order underpinning European colonization, provided crucial support to quasi-states. We can begin to explore this through an examination of norms. Contemporary international society assumes tacitly that 'quasi-states' should enjoy the formal privileges of membership associated with state sovereignty, notwithstanding their limited material statehood. This instils in contemporary international society the norm that the judicial (if not real) sovereignty of quasi-states should be preserved. Of course, as demonstrated forcefully by several cases of foreign interventions/invasions, this does not always prevent external powers from interfering physically, for example, in Cuba (1961), Czechoslovakia (1968), Grenada (1983), Panama (1989), Afghanistan (1979, 2001) and Iraq (2003). Nonetheless, preservation of judicial sovereignty constitutes a key normative tenet of contemporary international society. As Jackson explains, sovereignty 'remains a legal barrier to foreign interference in the jurisdiction of states. The basic norm of the United Nations (UN) Charter (Article 2) enshrines the principle of equal sovereignty and its corollary, the doctrine of non-intervention'.[24] Judicial sovereignty also distinguishes contemporary from erstwhile international societies where judicial sovereignty was not afforded to states displaying partial material statehood.[25]

This normative shift is related strongly to another underpinning of contemporary international society: the rise of self-determination as a tenet of the 'new sovereignty regime'.[26] This is the second theme we examine in the context of how contemporary international society supports quasi-states. Clapham argues that the new sovereignty regime 'required the articulation of new conceptions of nationalism and self determination, in which the "nation" was equated with the inhabitants of any territory created by European colonialism'.[27] As self-determination rose to become a key normative tenet of contemporary international society, so the ruling elites of quasi-states were endowed with greater legitimacy to predicate their rule on an ideology of internal state consolidation. This ideology proved to be a powerful tool to justify the often authoritarian rules employed to control newly established quasi-states, and was useful for delegitimizing, although not eliminating, external intervention.[28] Thus, although subject to foreign interference, the ruling elites in quasi-states escaped the prolonged colonization imposed on their predecessors. Moreover, in situations where quasi-states' material statehood virtually imploded – for example, during civil strife in Afghanistan, Lebanon, Burma, Chad and Angola – judicial sovereignty and the normative consensus on the right of self-determination were the remaining elements of statehood that prevented these imploded quasi-states from being totally extinguished.

At the same time, a measure of agency on the part of regimes within quasi-states is required to fully capture the enduring pathologies that shape this form of sovereignty. As Jean-Francois Bayart notes with respect to the African political elite, their remarkable ability to mobilize the material resources of the international community to serve their own domestic power struggles -- through recourse to ideology, humanitarianism and conventional economic and political needs of foreigners – has been a consistent theme across Africa's history.[29] These patterns and practices can be seen across time, from the dramatic shifts in ideological direction performed by various Ethiopian regimes and Angolan liberation movements during the CW, to the instrumentalizing of humanitarian crises by governments in Mozambique and opposition in the Democratic Republic of Congo in more recent years. Moreover, the argument that local political elites deliberately undermine constitutional states – that the 'chaos' and administrative malfunctions are instrumentally produced by them to ensure their grip on power and control – is presented forcefully in Chabel and Daloz's analysis of the African state.[30]

The support given by contemporary international society to quasi-states through judicial sovereignty, institutionalization of self-determination and delegitimization of prolonged foreign domination, is complemented by its endowment of development entitlements. Quasi-states have demanded (and received) assistance from international society to develop economically. This assistance has taken various forms, for example, aid flows, technical assistance, debt relief, humanitarian relief and refugee aid. This assistance and the 'rents' that quasi-states are able to extract from international trade, form a substantial part of the funds that these states use to finance their (partial) bureaucracies and state institutions.[31]

We examine the implications of notions of the quasi-state and its relationship with contemporary international society for conceptions of FPA, first by exploring how the external environment is conceived. FPA sees it in terms of the constraints it imposes on states. As mentioned earlier in reference to Elman's, Webber's and Smith's work, neo-realist and dependency formulations respectively highlight the exigencies imposed by politico-military and socio-economic international structures.[32] Pluralists underscore the complexities of foreign policy conducted in a mixed-state and non-state actor environment. Common to all these depictions is that they counterpoise the state and the external environment, the latter usually depicted as ominous. The notion of the quasi-state underlines that a different type of relationship can develop between the state and the external environment. In this relationship quasi-states are *supported* by and entwined with contemporary international society. Indeed, it is difficult to see how quasi-states can exist without the equal status afforded by judicial sovereignty through international law; without the political legitimacy endowed by the right to self-determination; and the material support granted by development entitlement over the years.

Furthermore, the quasi-state has important implications for how FPA conceives of the relationship between state, society and foreign policy. The previous section on the institutional state highlighted the liberal and societal approaches in FPA. We argued that the notion of the institutional state requires that we pay more attention to the relative autonomy of the state. The notion of the quasi-state, however, shifts the focus. As the institutional statehood of quasi-states is partial, they lack the kind of domestic structures underpinning institutional states. This should prompt a shift in FPA from an examination of how *formal domestic* structures affect foreign policy, to the effects on foreign policy of *informal domestic* arrangements, such as those that exist in quasi-states. By domestic structures, we mean 'the normative and organizational arrangements which form the "state", structure society, and link the two together'.[33]

Finally, the notion of the quasi-state has implications for how we conceive the foreign policy tools that states can exploit. FPA has recognized and accounted for a multiplicity of foreign policy tools states have at their disposal: the use of military force, economic and diplomatic sanctions, diplomacy, soft power, etc.[34] However, by dint of their partial material statehood, quasi-states' access to conventional foreign policy tools is limited or denied. At the same time, the security and development entitlements endowed by the institutional, normative and legal frameworks underpinning contemporary international society, grant access to different types of foreign policy tools. The scope of this chapter does not allow a discussion of how different states manipulate these resources and under what circumstances. However, we believe this would be a particularly fruitful avenue for FPA research.

The clustered state

This section explores the concept of the clustered state which derives from the work of historical sociologists on the implications of the political and military processes underpinning the so-called west since the onset of the CW.[35] The thrust of our argument hinges on a distinction between the intra-systemic and inter-systemic dynamics of the CW. Inter-systemic dynamics refers to the conflict between the US and the former USSR (and their corresponding blocs). Intra-systemic dynamics is the internal dynamics underpinning the west.[36] The west initially included North America, Western Europe, Japan and Australia. However, as the CW developed, the concept of the west extended to include parts of Latin America, the Middle East, Asia and Africa. In referring to intra-systemic dynamics we are including the political, economic, military and legal design underpinning the complex institutional framework of the west that emerged during the CW. This institutional framework includes political-military organizations (e.g. NATO), economic bodies (e.g. the International Monetary Fund (IMF), the World Bank), and a developing structure of global legal and enforcement institutions (such as international criminal tribunals). The institutional framework is complemented and buttressed by a system of bilateral and multilateral state alliances.[37]

The significance for this chapter of the institutional consolidation of the west lies in the statehood changes it entailed. We have discussed how the institutional conception of the state rests on the tacit assumption that states are territorially bounded entities, politically and militarily separate from each other, with each exerting a monopoly or at least some degree of control over the means of violence. However, the emergence of the west's institutional framework challenges these assumptions. It means that states *voluntarily*, though partially, pool their sovereignty and use of political force – at least in the external sphere – within a raft of established international politically integrated institutions.[38] This makes it more difficult to perceive states according to the institutional conception, namely, as discrete national units with clearly demarcated and mutually exclusive 'borders of violence'. By borders of violence we mean that borders are not just administrative divisions, but also lines along which violence could erupt.[39]

Laffey and Barkawi argue convincingly that the gradual pooling of authority and use of political force into a large number of international, politically integrated institutions, has eliminated borders of violence in the west, rendering it a zone of peace.[40] In this sense, the west can be perceived as politically integrated – so much so, that Shaw and others consider consolidation of the west's institutional framework to herald the emergence of a new, albeit embryonic, global state.[41] This claim appears flawed, however, particularly since it is based on Mann's institutional definition of the state. Recall that a central tenet of Mann's conceptualization is that states 'bind' territories by exerting despotic or infrastructural power. Those proposing the notion of a global state provide neither an empirical nor a theoretical explanation of how the 'western' institutional entity binds 'its' territory. We would suggest, therefore, that the notion of 'clustered state' better reflects the pooling of sovereignty and use of the means of violence in the institutional framework underpinning the west.

The notion of clustered state has three important implications for FPA. First, it implies a different type of state– society relations than those discussed above. It is precisely because sovereignty and control over the means of violence are voluntarily pooled by states that it is easier for social relations to operate across national borders. This results in linkage politics – a recurrent sequence of behaviour that originates in one state and is reacted to by another – potentially becoming a more salient factor for determining foreign policy.[42] There can be three categories of linkage politics: 1) *reactive* linkages, which occur when events in one society lead to spontaneous reactions in another, unprompted by governments; 2) *emulative* linkages, which emerge when an event in one society is quickly imitated by the citizens in another; and 3) *penetrative* linkages, which occur when there is a deliberate attempt on the part of some elements in one society to enter, influence and, on occasion, manipulate another.[43] Thus, within clustered states, both the domestic societal elements and the networks transcending the state boundaries they may create, matter.

The linkage politics effect has implications for how the external environment is conceived. So far we have discussed the external environment in terms of either the exigencies it imposes or the supportive effects it can generate, on which quasi-states depend. In both cases the external environment emerges as a *structure,* but in the clustered state the external environment is conceptualized differently. Since states are partially pooled, agency exists at multiple sites and involves numerous players: societal actors, governments, and a plethora of global and international institutions. The notion of the external environment involving multiple levels of agency has implications also for how FPA accounts for the foreign policy tools used by clustered states. The political and military pooling of clustered states makes them more prone than quasi- and institutional states to employ foreign policy tools multilaterally. This employment might take the form of joint military operations, for example, the 1990–91 Gulf War, and the war in Afghanistan since 2001, but it applies also to measures taken to shape the economic environments these states operate under, for example, steps taken to curb the global recession since 2008. Foreign policy in relation to the environment is another good example of clustered states employing foreign policy tools multilaterally. Successful foreign policy, under these circumstances, is oriented towards an ability to present aims in language that speaks to the normative values that inform clustered states and, therefore, can form the basis for collective action. The Bush administration's marked failure in this respect in early 2003 set the stage for the subsequent divisive foreign policy within the west.

Institutional, quasi- and clustered states: analytical implications for foreign policy

Having examined the notions of institutional, quasi- and clustered states we next explore some of the analytical implications of these conceptions for FPA, in order to identify links between these types of states and foreign policy. We do this under three themes: available foreign policy tools; source of state autonomy in the context of foreign policy; and inputs from the external environment.

Foreign policy tools

In terms of the foreign policy tools available to states there are marked differences between institutional, quasi- and clustered states.

Institutional states are the closest state form to what Weber and followers discuss as the modern state. Correspondingly, for foreign policy implementation, institutional states rely primarily on the foreign policy tools that accompanied the rise of the modern state: modern diplomacy, embodied by the institution of ambassador; exertion of military force by modern armies; economic instruments to consolidate inter-state relations or impose sanctions; balancing power and its dynamics via systems of alliances. States in the Middle East state system since the end of WWII are a good example of institutional states and their employment of modern foreign policy tools. At the time of writing the region is engulfed in a string of popular uprisings whose outcomes might change the nature of the state in the Middle East and the foreign policy tools used. However, since the end of colonialism in the late 1950s and early 1960s, until very recent times, the Middle Eastern state system exemplifies our argument about the connection between the institutional modern state and the type of foreign policy expected to be employed.[44]

As already mentioned, quasi-states have very different capabilities. Their partial or even non-existent state apparatuses do not endow the material capabilities enjoyed by institutional states to shape their foreign policy environments. The foreign policy tools available to quasi-states often derive from the strong links forged by the regime with international society, frequently the guarantor of their existence, as well as their ability to mobilize networks of support from elements in global civil society. For instance, the governing regimes in quasi-states work within international agencies (e.g. the UN, World Bank, IMF) to promote their interests and also may engage with the multiplicity of NGOs working with their countries; their relationships with these latter can vary from shared complicity of purpose to friction and opposition. NGOs may work to promote their agendas, for example, through the 'drop the debt' campaign in 2000 on behalf of African countries. They may argue for diplomatic support for embattled regimes, for example, conservative NGOs in Britain and the US in the context of apartheid in South Africa, maintaining that 'constructive engagement' would be a less violent route to political change than supporting the armed struggle promoted by left-leaning NGOs.[45] At other times, however, NGOs can be strongly critical of the policies of these states, especially in the area of human rights and service delivery to the poor. The dominant roles of foreign NGOs in many social services sectors during the extended national emergency in Mozambique from the mid-1980s into the 1990s was criticized by elements in government and by some foreign activists.[46] Although it is clear that in many humanitarian disasters the state's capacity to provide for the local population is extremely limited if not non-existent – there is nonetheless a self-serving character to some foreign relief organizations which seems (somewhat perversely) to thrive on state weakness.[47]

Clustered states, which exhibit elements of institutional states, but are more enmeshed in international and global structures, combine conventional use of modern foreign policy tools with a strong disposition towards multilateralism. Precisely because these states have voluntarily, although partially, pooled their sovereignty and authority in regional and sometimes global political frameworks, they are more inclined than modern states to engage in multilateral foreign policy. This is manifest in how they cooperate with other states on a variety of issues, in their frequent use of the myriad of global institutions to pursue their goals, and in their adherence to international law. Notwithstanding the tensions experienced by the European Union (EU), it is a prime example of the disposition of clustered states towards a multilateral foreign policy in the context of working with global institutions and heeding international law.

The relative autonomy of the state

As already mentioned, the institutional state derives its autonomy from its unique positioning to deal with the exigencies imposed by international security competition, its monopoly over the means of violence, its ability to conduct surveillance of its citizens, and its extractive apparatus, for example, system of taxation. It can be expected that foreign policy decision making and implementation will reflect these relatively autonomous dimensions of the state. The role played by the coercive apparatus – military and internal security services – is the chief embodiment of the autonomy of the state. The state exhibits autonomy from external and internal elements and, also, in the context of foreign policy, a relative autonomy from government. This relative autonomy generates tensions that are manifested in diverse ways, from innocuous leaks from 'state' or 'government' officials, to the most extreme case of government overthrow by the state in a military coup.[48] Thus, in the institutional state, foreign policy makers are required to manage the tensions generated by domestic societal sources, the state's relative autonomy and inputs from the external environment. We return to this theme later in this chapter.

While institutional states have a sophisticated state apparatus, including near monopoly over the means of violence, the state apparatus of quasi-states is partial at best. Thus, within the quasi-state the state's relative autonomy is related to regimes rather than whole states, which has an effect on foreign policy; their autonomy does not necessarily derive from the coercive means of violence and extraction. Extraction is derived not from a formal taxation system – the administrative apparatus to conduct this being too institutionally robust and complex – but rather through simpler rent-seeking conduct aimed primarily at foreigners and their corporate interests. Thus, the relative autonomy of quasi-states derives primarily from the regime's access to international society, the guarantor of the quasi-state. Access to aid and trade rents, and security guarantees from international society allow the regime, via its foreign policy, to increase its relative autonomy from societal forces. Hence, the dependence of the quasi-state on the external environment for maintaining its relative autonomy is more pronounced than in the case of an institutional state. Its foreign policy does not reflect a balance between response to societal pressure, external inputs and its relative autonomy; more likely, the linkage between the regime's relative autonomy and its dependence on access to external resources will override societal pressure. This lengthening distance between the quasi-state and society can be seen, for instance, in the aggressive imposition of harsh structural adjustment programmes upon populations by regimes in quasi-states whose primary source of legitimacy is derived externally, from the IMF, or the willingness to host foreign military forces to serve the regime's interests. Moreover, reflecting regime disengagement from local society, foreign policy becomes devoted essentially to managing these relations with external actors with little or no regard for the consequences on society as a whole.

The relative autonomy of clustered states is different again, in that it is conditioned by their embedding in international and global political institutions. However, unlike quasi-states, which are dependent on these political frameworks, clustered states and international/global institutions are in a mutually constitutive relationship. Thus, although the quasi-state is less independent of external influences than the institutional state, it is able to manipulate a position in the external environment that enhances its autonomy in relation to societal actors. Examples include the coordinated anti-terrorist legislation following the 9/11 attacks on the US, measures to prevent money laundering and the limits imposed on immigration, all means through which clustered states have enhanced relative autonomy through embeddedness in international/global political frameworks. Foreign policy is designed to both enhance the relative autonomy of the state from societal actors *and* shape the external environment such that it enhances this relative autonomy of the state.

The external environment

Differences in foreign policy tools and the relative autonomy of the state have implications for how, analytically, we conceptualize the external environment of clustered, institutional and quasi-states. We have discussed above that clustered states exhibit a mutually constitutive relationship with the external environment. This has important implications for how FPA conceives of the relationship between the foreign policy of clustered states and the scope and nature of the external environment. We explore this question in depth in Chapter 6, which looks at foreign policy and globalization. In the meantime, suffice to say that we conceive the foreign policy of clustered states and the external environment as mutually constitutive.

This does not apply to the institutional state. In the effort to maintain territorial sovereignty the institutional state is exposed mainly to the inputs generated by the external environment, and will play an insignificant role in shaping that environment. In other words, the national interest of the institutional state, however imperfectly defined, is shaped in the arena of the external environment, which, in turn is used by foreign policy to achieve specific goals. The institutional state responds to the inputs generated by socio-economic and military-political international structures, and the plurality of non-state actors and forces operating in the system.[49] Finally, the quasi-state's foreign policy is aimed neither at changing the external environment nor at its own specific environment. The aim of quasi-state foreign policy is to uphold the *supportive* role of the external environment in maintaining in place this quasi-state status and survival of the regime.

Conclusion

This chapter examined the epistemological, ontological, conceptual and analytical tensions generated by the lack of a conception of state in FPA. We addressed these tensions by reconciling the HS literature on the state, and FPA. We identified three state types: institutional, quasi- and clustered. We developed these different conceptions of state and examined their implications for FPA based on the degree to which they possess *material statehood*, that is, the institutions comprising states and the extent to which they have authority over binding rule making and political force. The discussion demonstrates that explicit conceptions of state have significant implications for key understandings in FPA. The sections in this chapter explored the implications of different conceptions of the state for FPA and how state–society relations impact on foreign policy. We looked at their impact on conceptualizations of the external environment and suggested new ways for rethinking how FPA understands why states exploit their foreign policy tools. We believe that the discussion in this chapter resolves some of the tensions inherent in FPA based on poorly articulated conceptions of the state. We hope that our argument extends the conceptual and analytical canvas and allows FPA to account more accurately for why different types of states pursue different foreign policies.

6 Foreign policy, globalization and the study of foreign policy analysis

Introduction

Although the term 'globalization' has been in academic use since the 1970s, no serious attempts were made to theorize it until the late 1980s. These attempts developed into a stimulating debate, comprising what Held et al., in their influential work *Global Transformations*, term globalization theory (GT).[1] Examination of what we deem to be the best-known works, and most popular forums on globalization, reveals that foreign policy[2] – the sum of the external relations undertaken by an independent actor (usually a state) as part of international relations – is virtually excluded from GT.[3] Similarly, as discussed in the introduction to this book, students of FPA usually exclude GT from its matrix. In our view, the mutual exclusion of FPA and GT is problematic. Foreign policy is seen usually as the quintessential 'boundary' activity, at the interface between the domestic and the external spheres. While these spheres have never been completely separate, the boundary between them seems to have become more porous as a result of globalization – *a multidimensional contested process that involves an increasing embedding of political, military, economic, social and cultural activities in politically unified (quasi) global spheres of activity.*

There are numerous manifestations of this trend. For example, since the end of WWII, states have become gradually more embedded in a plethora of multilateral, global political institutions and military organizations; 'national' economies increasingly are implanted into global economic arenas such as trade and finance; and the information technology revolution has made it very difficult for states to control information. This embedding has been forcefully illustrated in the controversy surrounding the dissemination of hundreds and thousands of classified diplomatic cables on the WikiLeaks website.

Throughout this book we have emphasized that foreign policy is an activity that has relative autonomy, deriving from the roles of the decision makers, bureaucratic politics or the state itself. Arguably, as an activity situated on the cusp between the domestic and external environments, foreign policy will have a formative effect on the activities occurring across the domestic–international–global nexus. In this context, the gap in contemporary IR theory, framed by the mutual theoretical and conceptual neglect of FPA and GT, is clearly significant.

The aim of this chapter is not to try to close this gap, but to achieve the more modest aim of deriving from GT a conceptualization of the possible role/s that foreign policy plays in the context of globalization. In our view, this would seem an essential first step towards facilitating a broader debate that brings together GT and FPA. It is to be hoped that such an encounter could lead the adherents to both bodies of literature reworking some key concepts in light of what we would suggest is the mutually constitutive impact of globalization and foreign policy. For example, within FPA the literature on decision making and bureaucratic politics assumes, if unwittingly, that the state is a bounded entity. Whilst globalization does not entail an unravelling of the state from above it does suggest, as we shall see, that states are pooling their sovereignty and authority to a greater degree than before. This means that decision making and bureaucratic politics are not merely located at the level of the national executive, but in some cases are embedded within global political frameworks. Referring to the classifications identified in Chapter 5, we would suggest that quasi- and clustered states are more exposed to this dynamic than are institutional states. A thorough examination of these implications is beyond the scope of this chapter, but we hope that our conception of the role/s of foreign policy in the context of globalization constitutes a concrete contribution towards a debate that will engage with these issues.

The first great debate on globalization: implications for foreign policy

Hyperglobalists vs. global sceptics

This section explores how the key approaches in GT – hyperglobalist, global-sceptic and transformationalist theses – conceptualize the causes, timeframe and impact on the state of globalization.[4] This discussion is geared towards ascertaining how and to what extent these theses might account for foreign policy in conditions of globalization.

We begin by examining the hyperglobalist thesis. This school of thought emerged within a scenario of two processes that seemed to sweep the world in the late 1980s and early 1990s: the revolution in information technologies, and the triumph of capitalism and a liberal democracy over rival political-economic models, for example, Fascism and Communism.[5] According to the hyperglobalist thesis, the emergence of a single global market, above all other factors, propels globalization. Correspondingly, globalization is conceived of as 'a new era in which peoples everywhere are increasingly subject to the disciplines of the global market place'.[6]

From this vantage point globalization is seen as having a significant impact on the state. John Gray, for instance, contends that as a result of globalization 'nation-states find themselves in an unfamiliar environment in which the behaviour of global market forces is decreasingly predictable or controllable'.[7] This, he argues, reduces the leverage of sovereign nation-states. Other hyperglobalists, such as Kenichi Ohmae, hold even more extreme convictions that 'economic globalization is constructing new forms of social organization that are supplanting, or that will eventually supplant, traditional nation-state as the primary economic and political units of world society'.[8]

By inference, the assertions made by the hyperglobalist thesis regarding the nature and scope of globalization, its causes and its impact on the state, have dramatic implications for foreign policy. Foreign policy, a quintessentially political activity, is rendered extinguished by technology and the emerging single market global economy. Thus, FPA, with its emphasis on the relative autonomy of foreign policy, is rendered incompatible with the hyperglobalist thesis, which would appear to reinforce the mutual exclusivity of FPA and GT.

The controversial arguments of the hyperglobalist thesis generated a wave of critical writings. One of the most forceful critiques came from what came to be known as the global-sceptic thesis.[9] The global-sceptic thesis sets out to critique a key hyperglobalist argument that the post-CW world heralded a new epoch in human history driven by the logic of a single market global economy and the information technology revolution. To this end, global sceptics compare economic data from the late nineteenth and twentieth centuries, for example, labour mobility across the globe, convergence of the world economy around a single currency and freedom of trade. Based on this comparison they conclude that the late twentieth century does not represent a fundamentally new era in the globalization of the economy. They contend that, in some respects, the late nineteenth-century world economy was more globalized than the later twentieth-century economy and that the former represented a new epoch in terms of the effects generated by new technologies; the inventions of the telegraph, the steamboat and steam trains in the late nineteenth century are identified as having generated similar if not greater social, economic and political effects to those produced by the IT revolution.

If globalization does not, as the hyperglobalists argue, represent a new era, then what does it reflect? Global sceptics contend that the hyperglobalist depiction of globalization is a myth designed to advance the institutionalization of the neo-liberal economic project.[10] They argue that this has resulted in the discourse surrounding globalization being framed by the assumption that the process has inevitable consequences, which states ignore at their peril. Global sceptics are especially critical of the hyperglobalist argument that the logic of the global single market is dictating the winners and losers among states.

What are the implications of an alternative sceptic account for international politics -- and particularly foreign policy? Global sceptics argue that what hyperglobalists call globalization is in fact an intensified phase in the internationalization of the world's powerful states and their economies. Internationalization, like globalization, refers to a growing interdependence between states, but internationalization assumes states continue to be discrete national units with clearly demarcated and mutually exclusive borders of violence.[11] Borders of violence means that borders are not merely administrative divisions, but boundaries across which conflict may emerge. Through this prism the state is conceived as entirely otherwise than in retreat. It is states, particularly the most powerful states, that define the scope and nature of globalization, rather than vice versa. In fact, the sceptics argue that contemporary internationalization reflects the political distribution of power among stronger and weaker states.

Conceptualizing the post-CW era as a form of internationalization rather than globalization entails a different notion of foreign policy than the hyperglobalist thesis. In contrast to the hyperglobalist account, foreign policy is not extinguished by the uncontrolled economic-technological forces driving globalization. Instead, by dint of its being a key state activity, foreign policy is at the heart of an essentially state-driven process of internationalization. Within this framework FPA would play a central role in explaining how foreign policy making and its implementation affect contemporary internationalization.

At first glance this idea might seem compelling. However, the global-sceptic account exhibits a number of weaknesses that would seem to undermine its core argument. First, the contention that in terms of the global economy and technological innovation the late nineteenth and late twentieth centuries are fundamentally similar, is predicated on an extreme Eurocentric view. For the global south, these periods are not comparable. In the late nineteenth century much of the global south was under European domination. However, since the end of the CW countries comprising the global south, for example, India, have become formidable players in the world economy and international politics. Thus, the claim that for countries in the global south the late nineteenth and twentieth centuries represent a somewhat similar situation is completely flawed.

Second, the global-sceptic account would seem to understate the degree to which the transnational environment surrounding states has become denser and more complex. The scope and nature of non-state actors – from NGOs and MNCs, to terrorist groups, diasporas and the environment, to global markets – presents to states an unprecedentedly dense and complex environment.[12] The global-sceptic account, however, underestimates this shift, providing an inaccurate conception of globalization, its causes and the possible implications for foreign policy. It does not seem useful, therefore, for FPA to adopt global-sceptic propositions as the basis for an examination of foreign policy in conditions of globalization/internationalization. Adopting a sceptic position could result in FPA, similar to the global-sceptic account, adopting an essentially Eurocentric view and understating recent changes in the transnational environment.

The transformationalist thesis: towards a third way?

The views within the global-sceptic thesis have prompted students of globalization to revisit the debate, resulting in a third strand focused on the first great debate in globalization: the transformationalist thesis. The transformationalist thesis critically scrutinizes the debate between the hyperglobalists and global sceptics on globalization, its causes and impact. As we mentioned in the introduction to this book, by the end of the 1990s this scrutiny had defined the contours of the first great debate on globalization and placed the transformationalist thesis at the forefront of what emerged as GT.[13] There are three claims underpinning the transformationalist account which are pertinent to the discussion here. We examine each in turn to clarify their implications for the activity of foreign policy in conditions of globalization.

The transformationalist thesis challenges the view that globalization is an economics-driven process and proposes instead that it is driven by a fundamental shift in the spatio-temporal constitution of human societies. For example, Held et al. define globalization as 'a process (or set of processes) which embodies a transformation in the spatial organisation of social relations and transactions – assessed in terms of their extensity, intensity, velocity and impact – generating transcontinental or interregional flows and networks of activity, interaction and the exercise of power'.[14] Scholte, in turn, perceives globalization as 'deterritorialization', or the growth of 'supraterritorial' relations among people.[15] Scholte emphasizes that globalization 'refers to a far-reaching change in the nature of social space'.[16] As noted earlier with reference to Rosenberg's work, transformationalists argue that the shift in the organization of time and space has been so profound that it has revealed a retrospective and basic lacuna in the classical, territorially grounded tradition of social theory, which requires a new, post-classical social theory to be developed, in which the categories of space and time assume central, explanatory roles.[17]

Based on this spatio-temporal conception of globalization and its causes, the transformationalist thesis provides an account of the impact of globalization on the state. Transformationalists stress the changes prompted by globalization, but recognize the state's capacity to adapt in the face of these changes and do not foresee a disappearance of the state from the various global arenas in which it operates. They emphasize also that, although not entirely controlled, globalization is strongly politicized and is state regulated.[18] Transformationalists prefer to discuss the trends generated by globalization in terms of a transformation of the state such that 'its powers, roles and functions are rearticulated, reconstituted and re-embedded at the intersection of globalizing and regionalizing networks and systems'.[19] Thus, they do not support the imminent demise of the state suggested by the hyperglobalists. Nor do they accept the global-sceptic view that the role of states in the global arena has remained essentially unchanged. Rather, the transformationalist thesis suggests that, in reorganizing time and space, globalization is redefining the territorial basis underpinning the political order of the sovereign nation-state, and its corresponding Westphalian international order, compelling states to transform and adapt.[20]

Although the transformationalist account of the impact of globalization on the state is more nuanced than the hyperglobalist and global-sceptic theses, it does not help to explain foreign policy in conditions of globalization. The problem lies in the fact that similar to the hyperglobalist thesis the transformationalist approach conceives of the state as external and counter-positioned to contemporary globalization. Also, foreign policy, as a key state activity and as a major embodiment of the state in the global arena, is rendered external and counterpoised to globalization. Furthermore, the ontological primacy that the transformationalist thesis attributes to time and space renders foreign policy subordinated in some essential way to the logic prescribed by the spatio-temporal processes driving globalization. In ontological terms, this formulation is problematic: it implies that most government political action not aimed at harnessing globalization is doomed to fail. It suggests also that traditional foreign policy, which tends to assume the primacy of the political, is subsumed by spatio-temporal processes and is barely relevant. Hence, the transformationalist thesis is somewhat fatalistic about the prospects for the political management of globalization and underestimates the degree of choice open to governments.[21] It follows from this that, viewed through the transformationalist prism, foreign policy and the study of FPA have virtually no role in the debate over globalization.

This perception is reinforced by how the transformationalist thesis conceives of the relationship between globalization and international politics – understood as the interactions among state actors, across state boundaries, that have a specific political content and character. The transformationalist thesis converges around the assumption that, at some historical junctures, most notably the late nineteenth century, globalization and international politics were mutually constitutive. For instance, Held et al. argue that 'the rapidly developing empires of Britain and of other European states were the most powerful agents of globalization'.[22] However, the transformationalist thesis suggests that international politics and globalization after the age of empire are at odds because the economic and spatio-temporal transformations generated by globalization corrode the contemporary *territorial-based* international system of states. Thus, Rosenau argues that globalization 'allows peoples, information, norms, practices, and institutions, to move about oblivious to or despite boundaries'.[23] The transformationalists argue further that contemporary 'non-territorial globalization generates a transformation that is replacing the Westphalian international order with a multi-layered system of global governance in which sub-state, inter-state, supra-state and private governance bodies operate simultaneously, beyond the confines of states'.[24] In these accounts, international politics (after the age of empire), predicated on the territorially based international system of states, is subsumed by non-territorial globalization. Foreign policy, a constitutive element within international politics, is perceived in similar terms.

A mutually constitutive thesis of globalization: implications for foreign policy

So far, the first great debate on globalization does not seem to contribute to the conceptualization of the possible role/s of foreign policy in the context of globalization. The hyperglobalist thesis implies that foreign policy is extinguished by economic and technological forces. The transformationalist thesis suggests that the state – and by extension foreign policy – is compelled to change according to the logic prescribed by a radical transformation in the organization of time and space. If globalization were to be understood as generating these types of conditions, it would be conceived as rendering foreign policy insignificant, leaving little room for FPA to contribute to our understanding of global processes.

We reject this suggestion. In the remainder of this chapter we rehearse an argument that should constitute a fourth thesis of globalization: the mutually constitutive thesis. This thesis builds on the body of knowledge drawn on in Chapter 5 to develop the notion of the clustered state.[25] Based on a three-pronged critique of the hyperglobalist and transformationalist theses, we argue that this literature constitutes the foundation for a mutually constitutive thesis of globalization. We explain this thesis with the aim of deriving the possible role/s of foreign policy in the context of globalization.

A first critique is that the transformationalist and hyperglobalist theses attribute ontological primacy to spatio-temporal and to economic elements respectively, in conceptualizing globalization and its causes. In contrast, a neo-Weberian view of the mutually constitutive thesis is not concerned with establishing ontological primacy, but considers globalization as a multi-centric, multidimensional and dialectical process constituted by political and military factors alongside other elements – economic, technological, ecological, social, etc. A neo-Weberian ontology, by denying primacy to any one element, allows foreign policy to be conceived as one among several constituents of globalization.[26]

A second criticism concerns the conceptualization of the relationship between globalization and the state. Hyperglobalists see globalization rendering the state increasingly irrelevant whilst transformationalists take the more moderate view that globalization compels states to transform. Thus, the hyperglobalist and transformationalist theses converge around the assumption that the state is external and counterpositioned to contemporary globalization. This conceptualization is rejected by the mutually constitutive thesis. Shaw, for instance, argues that 'globalization does not undermine the state but includes the transformation of state forms. It is both predicated on and produces such transformations'.[27] This claim encapsulates the perception of globalization–state relations in the mutually constitutive thesis of globalization. It considers that globalization is both predicated on and produces transformations within the state, in a relationship that renders the two mutually constitutive.[28]

This conceptualization is pertinent to our discussion because most accounts of foreign policy recognize that it is driven centrally by the state.[29] Correspondingly, if the relationship between globalization and the state is mutually constitutive, then *foreign policy and globalization are also mutually constitutive.* As an embodiment of state activity, foreign policy can be conceived as a key site of states' political actions whilst responding to the challenges and opportunities presented by globalization. Israel and Egypt offer interesting examples of how states might make use of foreign policy in the context of globalization. Both states carried out a dramatic shift in their traditional foreign policy, partly with the aim of using the shift to embed their countries' national economies in global spheres of activities. In the case of Egypt, the decision to sign and maintain its 1979 peace agreement with Israel, ending three decades of hostility and five wars, was inextricably linked to the aim of opening up Egypt's economy through the *infitah* reforms. Since then, Egypt's economy has relied more than in the past on foreign sources of income, for instance, US and foreign aid, tourism and growing levels of foreign direct investment. Israel's decision to engage in the Oslo Process with the Palestine Liberation Organization, after three decades of mutual negation, exhibits a similar logic. Initiating the peace process was inextricably linked with embedding the Israeli economy in global spheres of activity, particularly in creating the political conditions that allowed Israeli companies to penetrate emerging markets in Asia.[30]

The third critique within the mutually constitutive approach of the hyperglobalist and transformationalist theses relates to their conceptualization of the relationship between international politics and globalization. As noted above, the hyperglobalist and transformationalist theses concede that during the age of empire, globalization and international politics were mutually constitutive. However, the advent of non-territorial globalization counter-positions these elements. The mutually constitutive thesis of globalization proposes a different way to understand the interrelationship between globalization and international politics. Namely, since the age of empire,[31] to the CW, to the global war on terror,[32] international politics has had a dialectical effect of contributing simultaneously to globalization and fragmentation. Since the hyperglobalist and transformationalist theses focus on the fragmenting effects generated by international politics, we would highlight their constitutive role in globalization and the place of foreign policy in this process. We focus on the CW, because therein lie the sources of contemporary globalization and within it the formative role of foreign policy.

In Chapter 5 we suggested that the intra-systemic dynamics underpinning the CW gave birth to a political, military, economic and legal institutional framework that underpins the west. This institutional agglomeration constitutes what we term a global cluster. States comprising the grouping are described as clustered states. The emergence of the global cluster and the political-military forces driving this process are at the heart of our account of how international politics and globalization are mutually constitutive, especially in terms of explaining the shift from internationalization to globalization.

As already described, internationalization presumes that while social relations expand states remain *discrete* national units within clearly demarcated and mutually exclusive borders of violence. In these terms, the notion of internationalization espouses the effects generated by the expansion of social relations to the global scale during the consolidation of European empires. This period, as already noted, witnessed an expansion in social relations such that hyperglobalists and transformationalists consider it the starting point of contemporary, non-territorial globalization.

The mutually constitutive thesis of globalization emphasizes political-militarist processes and challenges the view that the age of empire was a form of non-territorial globalization. As Mann and others observe, the process of imperial consolidation was accompanied by the naturalization of civil societies into nation-states, 'caged by state sovereignty and boundaries'. Correspondingly, an inter-imperial order emerged in which *each* European nation-state empire was itself a world order exhibiting its own authority structure, trade regime, dominant language and culture.[33] Thus, the hyperglobalists and transformationalists might argue that during the consolidation of empires, social relations might have become global. However, as 'caged', 'border-power-containing', nation-state-empire forms, operating within an inter-imperial order, states remained discrete, bordered national units. This means that the expansion of social relations during the age of empire could not have been more than internationalization.

For globalization to emerge a change in the *political structure* of social relations was required. Such a shift entails erosion of the national discreteness of states separated by the demarcated and mutually exclusive borders of violence that characterized the nation-state-empire form and its corresponding international order. The gradual replacement of the inter-state imperial order by the global cluster generated that eroding effect. The emergence of this institutional framework prompted states voluntarily – if partially – to pool their sovereignty and use political force, at least in the external sphere, to form a raft of international political and military institutions. This worked to eliminate the borders of violence between states and prompted a pooling and coordination of authority and the use of political force in a range of international institutions. So much so, that states engaged in what Ikenberry and Deudney refer to as 'security co-binding' or an 'attempt to tie one another down by locking each other into institutions that mutually constrain one another'.[34] In the process of this erosion of state boundaries, states were 'uncaged' (to paraphrase Mann), and driven to reducing the 'statization' of their economies, societies and cultures.

As a result of the changing international political structure, the expansion of social relations to a global scale through the activities of private, sub-state and supra-state entities, was taking place within an altered international political context. The previous borders of violence between component states were eliminated, a raft of international politically integrated institutions was established, and an interlocking geopolitical and economic context bound a core group of capitalist liberal-democratic states. Under these conditions, and unlike the period of imperial consolidation, the expansion of social relations was not conditioned by a politically fragmented, international political framework. Instead, social relations expanded within a politically unified sphere generated by the global cluster of states. The term 'unified political sphere' does not suggest that this realm was free of political pressure. For instance, the fact that a plurality of states comprised this sphere generated some frictions. Differences in the west over the US war with Vietnam and its involvement in the 1973 Arab-Israeli war are two examples.

However, the global cluster is generally regarded as being politically unified given the pooling of sovereignty, the elimination of borders of violence and the instatement of a global layer of international institutions. It is against this political-military backdrop that the key finding of the transformationalist thesis – that the extensity, intensity and impact of globalizaiton increased since the end of WWII – needs to be understood. This expansion of social relations within an altered political space created the conditions for the rise of contemporary globalization.

Within this view, the rise of contemporary globalization takes on a different character to that depicted by the hyperglobalist and transformationalist theses. Spatio-temporal and economic-technological processes are not the key driving forces of the rise of contemporary globalization. It is the politico-military processes underpinning the emergence of the global cluster that lie at the heart of contemporary processes of globalization. In this account the significance of foreign policy is its contribution to defining the interface between international politics and globalization. A core group of liberal, capitalist and democratic states lies at the heart of the global cluster. As Mann and others argue, these states were united in terms of their global interests, and similar in terms of their capitalist and nation-state structures, and their trade and investment with each other dominated the world economy, all of which created a broad consensual foundation for negotiations over international arrangements.[35]

Under the pretext of modernization and development and, later, promotion of democracy, western states used foreign policy to produce and sustain liberal spaces.[36] Liberal space meant expanding economic and to a lesser extent political liberalism, with the purpose of creating democratic subjects, and institutions to administer them. In this respect foreign policy convergence within the core of the global cluster, around maintaining political-military pooling and expansion of liberal spaces, provided the necessary political-military conditions to sustain the global cluster and the resultant rise of contemporary globalization. By the same logic, contemporary globalization reinforces the foreign policy stance of political-military integration within the west and the expansion of liberal spaces.

Conclusion

This chapter examined globalization theory in terms of the role/s of foreign policy in the context of globalization. The key theses comprising the first great debate on globalization are unhelpful. The assumption in the global-sceptic account that contemporary globalization is merely an advanced form of internationalization suffers from a Eurocentric bias and also understates the density and complexity of the global environment in the first decade of the twenty-first century. The hyperglobalist and transformationalist theses of globalization are similarly not helpful. They render foreign policy respectively as insignificant or subordinated to the economic-technological and spatio-temporal forces they identify as underpinning globalization. Foreign policy, essentially a political activity, is rendered insignificant. Since it affords almost no significance to foreign policy in the context of globalization, GT in its current form leaves little room for FPA to contribute to our understanding of global processes and the role/s foreign policy might play in them.

Our proposed mutually constitutive thesis of globalization, on the other hand, opens a new agenda for foreign policy, globalization and the study of FPA. We do not conceive economic-technological or spatio-temporal forces as key factors prompting the rise of globalization. In fact, our approach is predicated on the assumption that it is unhelpful to assign ontological primacy to any one factor. Instead, we employed a neo-Weberian ontology, stressing the plurality of factors constituting globalization. Through this prism, we conceive of the causes and impact of globalization somewhat differently from how the hyperglobalists and transformationalists envisage this phenomenon. Globalization, the state, and by extension foreign policy, are not counter-positioned. Rather, there is mutually constitutive relationship between globalization, the state and foreign policy. In addition, the expansion of social relations *alone* does not account for the rise of contemporary globalization and its impact. Rather, it is the *convergence* between the expansion of social relations – economic, cultural technological – and the consolidation of a politically unified global cluster during the CW that gives rise to contemporary globalization and its impact. In other words the expansion of social relations has to be accompanied by a change in the political structure of social relations for globalization to emerge.

From this vantage point, foreign policy appears to have two formative roles in the context of globalization. First, it constitutes a key site for political action states might use to seize the opportunities and meet the challenges posed by globalization. Second, as a formative activity of international politics it shapes the interface between international politics and globalization. We have shown that the core liberal states comprising the global cluster pursued a coherent and consistent foreign policy stance that proved crucial in creating the conditions sustaining the global cluster and enabling the rise of contemporary globalization and its liberal-capitalist imprint. Admittedly, an examination of how foreign policy impacted on globalization in the context of the global war on terror might show that it generated a rather different effect. Nevertheless, we hope we have conveyed that ignoring foreign policy results in partial accounts of how globalization and international politics interact.

In placing foreign policy at the core of the production and reproduction of contemporary globalization, the mutually constitutive thesis of globalization has key implications for FPA. Through this prism, globalization emerges as a process that involves a much greater degree of human agency than the alternative theses of globalization would acknowledge. With human agency afforded a greater role in globalization, employing FPA and its insights on the processes of decision making would enhance our understanding of the causes and impact of globalization.

The mutually constitutive thesis of globalization also has a conceptual implication for FPA. Several notions in FPA – from decision making, through bureaucratic politics, to notions of the external environment – are informed (if implicitly) by the assumption that the state is a bounded entity. Of course, as Chapters 4 and 5 show, FPA sees the boundary between the domestic and external environments as porous, but the state is conceived of as a bounded actor, which as this chapter has demonstrated, is far from the case. The elimination of borders of violence within the global cluster, the pooling of sovereignty and authority, and the creation of a global layer of state institutions, suggests that states affected by globalization are becoming increasingly embedded in global spheres of activities. Arguably, this constitutes a context different from that obtaining when the core areas of FPA investigation were formulated during the CW. Therefore, FPA should reconsider some of its key conceptions and adapt them to an environment affected by the conditions of globalization. Lastly, FPA has much to contribute to the empirical study of foreign policy in the context of globalization as articulated by the mutual constitutive thesis. This research agenda could include such themes as the impact of globalization on the foreign policy of particular states, how states use foreign policy as a political site of action to capture the opportunities and seize the challenges globalization presents, and the role of foreign policy in shaping the scope and nature of globalization.

7 Foreign policy and change

Introduction

Change is a neglected aspect of the study of foreign policy. Similar to the field of IR, which famously was not able to account for the rapid events that precipitated the ending of the CW in 1989, FPA tells us little about the sources and conditions that give rise to significant alteration to state foreign policy. This shortcoming is highlighted by Charles Hermann in his call for a greater integration of 'change and dynamics in theories of foreign policy',[1] and despite a few theoretical developments since then, this statement, by and large, still holds. This failure to incorporate change into FPA is important and, amongst other things, undermines the disciplinary claims that FPA enables deeper interpretation of international politics through its focus on the foreign policy process.

The relatively static depiction of foreign policy in much FPA in part is a reflection of the field's primary concern for decision making as process. The state and its foreign policy institutions are seen by academics essentially as given and timeless, subject to no more than incremental change. The only areas of FPA scholarship that, at least notionally, recognize that these conditions do not always hold are those concerned with the impact of crisis conditions on foreign policy decision making. These works tend to assume (notwithstanding US Secretary of Defense Robert McNamara's comments that all foreign policy is crisis management), however, that with the reversion to 'normalcy', established procedures and their concomitant structures reassert their places in the foreign policy process.[2] In related fields, such as political science and international political economy, which address aspects of foreign policy change, foreign policy is not necessarily seen by those outside IR as being tied to FPA while FPA practitioners are not aware of the work on foreign policy change outside their narrow disciplinary ambit. Recognizing and integrating the insights derived from these various sources is crucial for a fuller understanding of the process of change and its impact on foreign policy.

There have been several definitions proposed for the notion of change in relation to foreign policy. In general, foreign policy change comprises two main types of change: tactical and strategic. Tactical change in state foreign policy – what Hermann describes as adjustment and programme change – constitutes shifts within the established framework of policies that focus mostly on methods and instruments. Strategic change – described by Hermann as problem/goal and international orientation – involves more fundamental shifts in foreign policy based on a re-examination of foreign policy goals and the state's position in the international system.[3] Examination of the place of change in foreign policy can be achieved by analysing the change and its impact at the levels of the individual, of state institutions and of the political regime, which shed light on different aspects of the process. The role of agency, usually embodied in an individual actor, is a common thread in all these accounts. At the same time, these approaches have some limitations that call for consideration of constructivism as a source for understanding the meaning and process of foreign policy change.

The individual and change in foreign policy

An explicit focus on the role of the individual and change in foreign policy is quite novel. David Welch's work, *Painful Choices: A Theory of Foreign Policy Change* (2005), is one of the few efforts to broach this topic systematically. Welch tries to understand the diverse sources of foreign policy change by examining a set of approaches ranging from cognitive and motivational psychology to organizational theory and prospect theory. Underpinning the broad perspective adopted by Welch is the belief that change in foreign policy is not common and, when it does occur, is in direct relation to the decision makers' perceptions of loss.[4] In other words, change is most likely to occur in situations where foreign policy decision makers are fearful that continuing with the prevailing approach will likely come at a considerable cost. Welch says that:

> foreign policy is most likely to change dramatically when leaders expect the status quo to generate continued painful losses. States will not alter their behaviour simply to try to realize some marginal gain. The clearest signals of an impending change are

desperation, stridency and distress. The choice for change will often carry with it a risk of even greater loss – a risk of loss so great that, in many cases, no rational actor would accept it.[5]

Taking this statement as his point of departure, Welch reasserts the roles of the individual and of psychological factors in the decision-making process that is at the centre of an analysis of the sources and impacts of change on foreign policy. He suggests that this approach sidesteps the necessity to understand the structural impediments imposed by states, regimes and norms on individuals in dismissing all state behaviour as the product of human decisions.[6] His assertion of human agency as the single object of an analysis, that the international system is essentially static and that the study of international politics needs only to develop a generalized theory of change to capture the requisite characteristics of international politics, in many respects is too narrow. The emphasis on individual agency and insufficient recognition of the structural autonomy that institutions and normative practices assume – irrespective of their being generated and staffed by human beings – limits the interpretative power of what otherwise is an important corrective to the FPA literature.

Linking Welch's insights to the work of role theory on the foreign policy orientations of leaders suggests that the possibilities for foreign policy change reside in the particular personality traits of certain leadership types when confronted by challenging circumstances.[7] Although these types of leaders are subject to structural constraints at both the domestic and regional or systemic levels, the leadership role is central to the determination of a state's foreign policy. For instance, an 'expansionist' foreign policy orientation could likely respond better to the prospects of loss through the pursuit of a radical reorientation of foreign policy than a 'mediator-integrator' oriented strategy. Charismatic leaders (although this trait does not feature explicitly in role theory) are able to mobilize societies to support a range of otherwise controversial and costly foreign and domestic policy objectives.[8] John F. Kennedy's assertions that Americans would 'pay any price, bear any burden' in the pursuit of an activist foreign policy of containment of communism around the globe was echoed in Fidel Castro's commitment of Cuba's support of various revolutionary movements in Latin America and Africa.

However, there is clearly further scope for assessing the role of change in foreign policy. Drawing on relevant scholarly sources, in the literature on 'learning' there are insights into the part that individual leaders play in facilitating the foreign policy choices that embrace change.[9]

Inspired by the evident part played by Mikhail Gorbachev in instigating major change in the Soviet Union's foreign and domestic policies, scholars have sought to assess the degree to which decision makers engage in learning, and the extent to which they integrate what they have learned into their strategic thinking and action in relation to foreign policy. In line with the work on social learning in psychology, learning is a substantive departure from a previous position, or adaptation, or a tactical shift in foreign policy conduct: much of the debate in this literature focuses on these distinctions.[10] This account privileges sharp, dramatic changes in foreign policy while downplaying the possibilities of gradual change, over an extended period, which may result in equally fundamental shifts in foreign policy

The kind of incremental socialization that is presently infiltrating China's foreign policy, for example, is not well captured by conventional approaches to learning. According to Wang Jisi, China's foreign policy has undergone incremental change, through a series of four steps accomplished over a period of several years: adoption of a new definition of security, an orientation to multilateralism rather than bilateralism, the impact of economic development and changes to elite values.[11] The summative effect of this cautious and deliberative process is a Chinese grand strategy for the twenty-first century. In this context, a focus on leadership as the main agent of foreign policy change rather than political regimes (or, in the case of China, a political party) and changing institutional practices, masks the sources of change and the process by which it occurs. Moreover, it is clear that the division between learning and adaptation obscures the active interplay between policy formulation and implementation, which produces a continuous feedback loop in the actual practice of foreign policy.[12] The gradualist transformation of European foreign policies produced the Maastricht Treaty and the establishment of the European External Action Service (both instigated by choices made at the top, but strongly embedded via the functionalist integration approach adopted by the earliest institutional manifestations of the European Union), are examples of institutional forms of foreign policy change.[13]

One dimension of learning in foreign policy that has received scholarly attention is the use of history by decision makers. According to Yaacov Vertzberger, foreign policy decision makers are 'intuitive historians' who turn to history to manage complexity and identify policy alternatives.[14] Historical analogies are employed as framing devices to help decision makers identify the foreign policy situations they face – the proverbial 'definition of the situation' – and possible policy solutions.[15] While some presentations of foreign policy analogies from history are designed primarily to mobilize the public – the most frequent being the 'Munich analogy' applied by western leaders to support aggressive foreign policy action against non-democratic states – it would be a substantial misinterpretation to understand all such applications of history as merely instrumentalist. Yoon Foong Khong argues persuasively that foreign policy decision makers resort to historical analogies to fulfil a number of cognitive functions as well as to help them define situations, assess the political stakes and suggest possible solutions. Historical analogies have also been used to evaluate policy prescriptions on the basis of predicted outcomes, evaluate moral quality and provide warnings of potential dangers.[16]

A leader's search for foreign policy options that simultaneously provide insights into international events and the possibilities for their positive resolution can set a new course for state foreign policy. From this perspective, history does much of the 'hard work' involved in the foreign policy decision-making process by providing a reservoir of meaningful experience that facilitates the interpretation of international politics and from which plausible policy options can be constructed, while concurrently managing risk for the decision makers and providing an emotional crutch in situations of deep political uncertainty.

State institutions, domestic structures and foreign policy change

The important part played by state institutions in the foreign policy process – whether the formulation, interpretation or implementation of policy – has been acknowledged in the chapters in this book. Theories of bureaucratic politics emphasize the agency of state institutions in the foreign policy decision-making process; other theory is exploited to examine the influence of state institutions on foreign policy through the implementation of foreign policy aims.[17] However, the seminal work on state institutions – Allison's bureaucratic politics – strongly suggests that there are structural obstacles to change that are embedded within the routines and processes adopted by organizations. This assessment of foreign policy institutions, while appropriate for a number of cases and settings, is too one-dimensional. In the broader context of foreign policy change, state institutions can be the actual sources of change in foreign policy and sites for competition over new foreign policy ideas advocating change and their attendant new strategies.

Domestic structures can provide clues to the possibilities of change and the obstacles to change within a given polity. The distribution of authority between state and society, working through the operational constraints of domestic institutions and politics, is an important part of assessing not only when foreign policy changes, but the process of change itself.[18] For Holsti, foreign policy restructuring is as dependent upon the degree to which the state is involved and 'penetrated' by the external environment, as it is upon the person of the leadership and the nature of the policy-making process.[19] Holsti's inclusive approach to foreign policy change anticipates many of the insights that are the basis of neo-classical realism.

An integrative account of state institutions, domestic structures and foreign policy change draws on the literature on norm cycles and identity politics in relation to foreign policy change. Barnett's analysis of how skilful 'policy entrepreneurs' are able to re-frame identity issues within a specific institutional context in order to embark on dramatic foreign policy shifts, provides a theoretically eclectic treatment of foreign policy change which reasserts the role of agency.[20] It is the policy entrepreneur's ability to recognize opportunities created by crises and systemic developments that serve to discredit existing foreign policy approaches and open up space for new ideas, a reorientation of goals or a reconsideration of methods. Blavoukos and Bourantonis point out that it is not inevitable that crises induce the jettisoning of 'orthodox' foreign policy and its replacement with radical new approaches. Policy entrepreneurs are motivated by a willingness to accept that significant gains may not be immediately realized and it is their capacity to work within the constraints of prevailing domestic parameters to achieve these aims that distinguishes them.[21]

Joe Hagan's investigation into the strategies adopted by leaders to retain power – for example, mobilization, insulation and accommodation – within the competitive environment of domestic politics demonstrates how the nature of the domestic structure and the position of political actors within that structure, exercises a determining significant impact on the responsiveness of governments to these systemic-level drivers of foreign policy change.[22] In some cases, policy entrepreneurs can alter the institutional constraints to change posed by domestic structures, and consolidate the proposed foreign policy changes, by means of national referendums or constitutional reforms.

From a different angle, the sources of *resistance to change* within state institutions may be related to the level of bureaucratic embeddedness in the decision-making process, through the roles played by socialization, procedural scripts and cultural rationales.[23] Judith Kaarbo's work delineates the conditions under which bureaucratic minorities are able to resist change, for instance, by mobilizing procedural rules and practices to delay or distort the original intentions of particular policies which they see as being in some way against their interests.[24]

One example of bureaucratic resistance to foreign policy change was the deliberate thwarting of French President François Mitterrand's commitment to dissolve the Ministry of Cooperation, seen by many academic and political observers as a reservoir of paternalist colonial practices and networks that damaged French national interests.[25] Mitterrand, the leader of the Socialist Party, was elected president in 1981, swept into office partly as a result of the scandal surrounding the close links of his predecessor with a reviled African dictator, the self-styled Emperor Bokassa. His attempts to dissolve the Ministry of Cooperation were unsuccessful. Despite the appointment of a recognized critic to lead the Ministry of Cooperation, the ability of the ministry's bureaucrats to resist institutional change and, concurrently, to mobilize African support to oppose these fundamental alterations to the structure of Franco-African relations and also support from within Mitterrand's political circles, the process was doomed. Significant institutional change took another 30 years.

Under some circumstances, state institutions can serve as sites for both competing ideas on foreign policy and direct confrontation between competing domestic political actors. An excellent example of this was the experience of the incoming African National Congress (ANC) government in post-apartheid South Africa. The majority of the bureaucrats in the Department of Foreign Affairs (DFA) had been appointed by the National Party – the party that had promulgated apartheid – which meant that the initial residual resistance to implementing ANC policy prescriptions was inevitable.[26] This was despite the fact that there had been significant contact in advance of the forming of a government of national unity in April 1994, including a conference, which provided an opportunity for joint-framing of post-apartheid foreign policy and produced a remarkable degree of convergence of views on a range of international topics.

One of the areas where there were differences, however, was recognition of previous important ANC allies during the armed struggle, namely Cuba, Libya and the People's Republic of China. ANC appointees to the DFA, while better connected to President Nelson Mandela, leader of the ANC, were struggling to acclimatize themselves to government bureaucratic procedures and, in the context of a government of national unity, were obliged to work alongside apartheid-era bureaucrats. The latter had a distinct advantage in terms of their familiarity with established procedures, and were able to manipulate it to block foreign policy initiatives from above. For instance, the top

National Party-appointed civil servant within the DFA was in favour of retaining ties with the Republic of China or Taiwan, and reportedly used his senior position to block discussion at higher levels within government of any positions advocating a switch to recognition of the People's Republic of China.

Individuals are not the only foreign policy actors that can learn from history: foreign policy institutions also actively engage in learning, through the self-conscious establishment of 'lessons learned' units within state ministries of foreign affairs and defence ministries, and the UN Department of Peacekeeping Operations. The core of the military sciences is founded on an institutionalized form of learning from history through a curriculum involving constant review (and refighting) of historical military events and practices. In this context, the role of military academies and leaders drawn from that tradition deserve greater scholarly attention. These institutions' incrementalist responses to perceptions of threat – through curriculum development, training programmes or other learning outcomes – demonstrate a measure of commitment to incorporating change within the confines of organizational structures.[27]

'Epistemic communities', the network of knowledge-based experts who share a common outlook, methodology and set of normative commitments, are linked to institutionally based foreign policy change.[28] The ability of these communities to manage the highly technical requirements of a particular subject area – for example, nuclear armaments and programmes – provides them with a potentially high level of influence over key foreign policy decisions. As was demonstrated in debates over the expansion of arms programmes in the US and Europe in the 1980s, and in the build-up to the invasion of Iraq in 2003, these experts can have a significant impact on foreign policy choice.[29]

In this respect, institutional theory can be usefully applied to FPA, since it provides a depiction of the relationship between political behaviour and institutional impact and the structuring of foreign policy choice.[30] An in-depth examination of institutional theory and accompanying debates is beyond the scope of this chapter, but the 'principal-agent' debate is particularly interesting for FPA because of its insights on state conduct and international institutions. Principal-agent theory points to the limits of the principals' interests and influence over an implementing agent based on the former's information and preferences.[31] The scholarship on the UN and regional organizations such as the EU, suggest that these international institutions accrete increasing levels of autonomy from the very principals – states – that established and 'people' them and that these institutional 'agents' use an array of instruments ranging from legal, normative to procedural rules to affect foreign policy decision making and outcomes of principals.[32] The tension between the interests and preferences of these two categories of foreign policy actors form the basis of the bargaining and negotiation that accompany foreign policy formulation in multilateral organizations and, as such, produce discernable impacts on foreign policy. Change in the conduct of foreign policy based on the structural impediments imposed by international institutions is one obvious effect (and is reminiscent of the bureaucratic politics perspective), but it can also induce normative change in a particluar state's foreign policy through the pressure to subscribe to collective values in relation, for instance, to colonialism, democracy or human rights.

Political regimes and foreign policy change

Another approach to understanding foreign policy change is to examine it through the prism of political regimes. While studies of foreign policy realignment in response to systemic pressures to change suggest the saliency of domestic structures as a key determinant of regime responsiveness to such influences, the onset of structural regime change within a given country is a more obvious condition for foreign policy change. This formative shift from authoritarianism to democracy introduces new actors, ideologies and institutional imperatives into the policy process. These factors contribute to a re-examination of the core values of a state's foreign policy and, under certain circumstances, can produce new foreign policy orientations and outcomes. Understanding foreign policy change, from this perspective, involves examination of the relationships between regime type and socio-political changes in conjunction with broader systemic factors.

The foreign policy of transitional states, that is to say states moving from authoritarianism to democracy, has received relatively little attention from scholars in FPA. This is in spite of the fact that the wave of democratization that swept the globe in the latter half of the twentieth century, and over 40 countries experiencing the transition to democracy since the 1970s. Furthermore, with the collapse of the Soviet Union and Yugoslavia, a dozen new states – some of which are nominally democratic – emerged alongside states such as East Timor and Eritrea. Nevertheless, the foreign policy of transitional states arguably is one of the most interesting phenomena to study in terms of its insights into many of the theoretical concerns of the discipline and the character of the contemporary international system, as well as its varied empirical content. In particular, the study of the foreign policy of transitional states brings into sharp focus the agency and structure problem, the dynamic between state and non-state actors in the context of change and, finally, the socially constructed nature of sovereignty and the international system.

A rationalist account of foreign policy and transitional states consciously builds upon the comparative politics tradition and, in that sense, represents a break with the domestic orientation of this approach. The central questions that proponents of this tradition seek to answer in studying the foreign policy of transitional states are *when* do transitional governments pursue certain foreign policies over others, and *why*. To investigate these concerns, rationalist scholars employ classical insights derived from pluralist politics which focus on domestic structure and the relationship between interest groups and the state, as well as mechanisms of influence in policy making.

Samuel Huntington and Juan Linz, amongst the first scholars to tackle this topic, propose a typology of regimes as a guide to the foreign policy of transitional states.[33] First, transformation (incumbent caretaker) led from above; second, replacement (revolutionary provisional) in which the *ancien régime* is ousted completely by a revolutionary government, albeit with an explicit mandate to usher in democratic change; and third, transplacement (power-sharing interim government). Huntington and Linz suggest that each of these transitional governments faces a dilemma regarding the previous authoritarian government's foreign policy, specifically:

- how and when to demonstrate change;
- how and when to ensure continuity;
- how to retain or build legitimacy.

At the heart of this dilemma is the issue of to which constituency the government is beholden and/or should address in defining and making foreign policy choices. Huntington and Linz see these choices in stark terms, with transitional governments needing to balance their relationship with the international community with the need to address and secure a relationship with their domestic constituencies. Complicating the picture is the fact that the respective actors are not uniform in shape or outlook, with the international community divided among competing states, and the domestic environment characterized by factionalism.

Allison Stanger, building on this approach, focuses on regime type as the key determinant for understanding foreign policy choice by transitional governments. She says that the character of each of the three

regime types described by Huntington and Linz provides the underlying motivation for their foreign policy.[34] For example, because an
incumbent caretaker regime is fundamentally contiguous to the former
authoritarian government, it approaches foreign policy from the perspective of a search for outcomes that will be the least disruptive
and de-legitimizing to the interim governing arrangements. Thus, this
regime's foreign policy is characterized by continuity with the past.
A *revolutionary-provisional regime* seeks to promulgate a foreign policy
that demonstrates a clean break with the previous government. Thus,
its foreign policy is characterized by change from the past. Finally,
a *power-sharing interim government*, which is composed of a balance of
old and new elites and is influenced to a greater degree than the two
previous regimes by external forces, makes its foreign policy choices
around the particular circumstances posed by these dilemmas for
this balance. Thus a power-sharing interim government's foreign policy
is characterized by contingency.

Paulo Gorjao takes a different tack and explicitly introduces the role
of domestic politics into his study of foreign policy and transitions.[35]
He expresses dissatisfaction with the focus on regimes, pointing out
that this approach only partially answers the questions as to why and
when certain foreign policies are adopted by transitional governments.
He looks to domestic structure and, in particular, the role of corporate
(or institutional representations of collective interests) entities, such as
the military or the Roman Catholic Church, and charismatic individuals, to shape selection of and promote their respective interests on
foreign policy issues. His position is that in turbulent times of transition, these entities are better able to articulate and influence decision
makers who otherwise might lack the requisite information or the sense
of certainty needed to make difficult decisions. Furthermore, the conditions of transition facilitate more fluid access to elites and allow
for greater influence over foreign policy formulation by determined
domestic actors.

Additional research into states in transition to democracy suggests
that they are more likely than consolidated democracies to pursue
aggressive foreign policies. Mansfield and Snyder examine the conduct
of transitional states over a 200-year period and conclude that demo-
cratizing states are subject to formative nationalism and, given the
unstable conditions that accompany the instalment of new regimes and
the uncertainties surrounding boundaries of territory and citizenship,
engage actively in belligerent foreign policy approaches that reflect
these transitional tensions.[36] Indeed, as the cases of Serbia and Croatia
in the 1990s vividly demonstrate, the maxim that democracies never

fight one another does not hold for states in transition or for newly formed democracies.[37]

All these attempts to conceptualize and understand the foreign policy of transitional states, admirable though they may be in recognizing and accounting for foreign policy change, nonetheless suffer from the same basic shortcomings. The weakness of the rationalist approach to which they subscribe is rooted in the underlying assumptions that inform its ontology and, consequently, impact upon its particular epistemology. To wit, the state is held to be a priori, which is to say that there is no sense of it being the product of social forces and historical circumstances. Another aspect of the rationalist approach which is problematic is the fact that it does not account for intersubjectivity in terms of institutions and the processes that they represent and impart. A third problem is that the role of ideas is not clearly understood or articulated in relation to actors and institutions. To paraphrase one scholar, not only do ideas not float freely, they are deeply embedded in historically conditioned structures and contexts. Although rationalists do introduce the notion of identity through the neo-liberal ontology – norms, values, etc. – the manner in which they do so is not wholly convincing. Goldstein and Keohane, whose work on the role of ideas in IR paved the way for a rationalist reading of this dimension, do little more than treat identity as a new variable not previously accounted for.[38]

Scholars of the revolutionary state, whose focus necessarily involves upheaval and change, have sought to explain the impact of this condition on foreign policy and the international system.[39] For Fred Halliday, the paradox of established interpretations of the foreign policy of the revolutionary state rests with the contrasting accounts of its position on internationalism and nationalism. Halliday maintains that 'Revolutionary states conduct foreign policy within the space defined by two constraints – the impulsion to promote conflict and revolutionary change abroad, and the necessity of preserving and consolidating the revolutionary state at home'.[40]

On the one hand, the revolutionary state promulgates idealist foreign policies reflecting the underlying values of revolutionary solidarity. These run in parallel with – and are at times indistinguishable from – nationalist concerns. Nationalism can be a genuine expression of the revolutionary elites' outlook, as in revolutionary France's deeply nationalist foreign policy or Mao's Sino-centric vision of international politics. In other cases this nationalist impulse is more crudely instrumental, expressing the need to gain legitimacy from the domestic constituency, especially in the face of the mounting costs of 'adventurism' in foreign policy. The decision in 1976 of the then newly ensconced liberation movement in Mozambique, Frelimo, to sever all ties with white-ruled Rhodesia – an act of international solidarity with that country's liberation movements – came at tremendous economic cost and increased the alienation of the peasantry and local elites in adjoining central provinces, paving the way for counter-revolutionary forces to enter Mozambique.[41] Other factors curbing revolutionary-oriented foreign policies are the putative socializing effects of the international system, especially in the area of international finance, critical for newly established regimes intent on improving their domestic economies and citizens' livelihoods, and which shore up regime legitimacy.[42]

Quasi-states and cluster states and foreign policy change

The aforementioned depictions of the political regimes and their relationship to foreign policy of states in transition is grounded in rationalism which, with its emphasis on procedural rules and reductionist motivations, tends even in this volatile context to give a relatively static picture of the state and decision making. One of our central contentions in this book is that FPA lacks an explicit theory of the state and, in an effort to address this deficiency, we have proposed the notion of the quasi-state and the cluster state as more appropriate contemporary units for analysis of foreign policy.

The quasi-state, as described in Chapter 5, is a formal structure whose very institutional resilience is severely compromised by the contingencies of everything from administrative incapacity to deliberate political exigencies by local elites. These factors ensure the mutability of the quasi-state to elite and societal pressures or the demands of international legitimacy. The contingent character of the quasi-state makes it especially able to avoid the development of any of the institutional density that would accrue through adherence to recognized routines and transparent practices. Its openness to being re-inscribed with a changing set of rules and rationales by local elites means that it is particularly influenced by domestic forces and, at least in so far as local elites are able to recognize and respond to them, international systemic forces. The foreign policy implications of regime survival are an adaptive approach to those international issues tied to core questions of legitimacy, such as a strong commitment to the maintenance of the sovereignty principle, but paradoxically an inability to fulfil any of the substantive sources of legitimacy.

The cluster state is also structurally fitted to respond to change but in its case, the sensitivity to systemic sources of change is not a product of the shallowness of state institutions but rather their tensile strength. Tied to a myriad of international epistemic networks, globalized production chains and offshore platforms, dependent upon the global market to source vital materials and sell its products, simultaneously operating within regional bodies and sectorally defined groupings of states, the cluster state is wholly embedded in the globalization process. The cluster state is deliberately porous in its structures, reflecting an acute sensitivity to systemic change, and is as such adaptive and innovative in its foreign policy. Indeed, change is encoded into its DNA and, like a shark that needs to constantly move in order to breathe, any ossifying of institutions or a breakdown of the consensus over its commitment to embrace globalization holds the potential for crisis.

Towards a constructivist approach to foreign policy change

An examination of foreign policy change through the three prisms of the individual, state institutions and political regimes, provides some of the foundational pillars required for the development of a theory of foreign policy change. However, the artifice of these divisions, which is premised on atomized individuals and abstracted notions such as the state, in an effort to isolate critical variables within a positivist framework, imposes restrictions on their usefulness for FPA scholars. In this regard, constructivism, with its focus on mutually constituted identities, social practices and institutions, is in many ways more readily adapted to integrating change into its approach to international politics than other schools of thought in IR.

This is seen most clearly in our examination of foreign policy change in transitional states, which highlights constructivist insights into foreign policy as being integral to national identity construction at the same time as allowing for a range of contingencies to impact upon the process and foreign policy outcomes of the transition. Employing constructivism provides a means to account for the interplay between ideas, agents and structures, all of which are in a condition of flux and act as sources of influence on foreign policy.

To be specific, in the context of transitions, the points of access to policy makers within domestic structures effectively widen as consensus on procedures starts to be questioned or breaks down altogether. Foreign policy bureaucratic influence invariably is much reduced during transitions – although, at times, contingencies and idiosyncratic factors, as Gorjao suggests, can elevate and temporarily exaggerate an institution – while charismatic leadership plays a critical role in setting foreign policy agendas.[43] In such a volatile context, it is our view that *ideas* hold sway to an unprecedented degree, as institutions are ungrounded (authoritarian structures from the previous regime) or untested (incoming regime), with the result that it is principles that matter and become the critical currency of political dialogue. The degree to which individuals (charismatic leaders) and political parties are able to clothe themselves in these ideas/principles becomes the measure of success within an uncertain domestic and international constituency. Foreign policy issues and positions are considered in these terms, with little reference to materialist (power/capability) concerns or the implications of the norms, structures and legal framework of state action within the international system. Indeed, since the transitions by nature are based upon narrow elites often detached from the societies and the established structures of governance that they purport to represent, the scope for contingency is greater than might otherwise be the case. For example, a personality can assume heightened influence over the process based on his or her proximity to power or, in a power vacuum, because of a fluid domestic situation or uncertainty in the international sphere.

Within a post-transitional or consolidating government, however, the process of change is slowed or even abandoned as a touchstone of legitimacy. Routines begin to replace ad hoc decisions rooted in charismatic decision making as bureaucracies come to be the primary actor interfacing with the international legal system/multilateralism. Patterns of state–societal interaction are established through new constitutional structures, building upon the bargaining and compromise that characterized the negotiation period. The access points to power are formalized and informal networks are routinized, making the societal influences over foreign policy less subject to ideas-based contingencies or factors such as personal charisma.

Based on the insights of so-called 'thick' constructivists, the place of foreign policy change becomes more consequential (even primordial) than the above reading of constructivism. In this regard, David Campbell's work deepens our understanding of foreign policy and change. Campbell sees the paramount task of foreign policy to be the construction of identity through formative nationalism manifested in the very act of foreign policy.[44]

> all states are marked by an inherent tension between the various domains that need to be aligned for an 'imagined community' to come into being – such as territoriality and the many axes of identity – and the demand that such an alignment is a response to (rather than constitutive of) a prior and stable identity ... The

constant articulation of danger through foreign policy is thus not a threat to a state's identity or existence: it is its condition of possibility.[45]

However, because Campbell's insights are derived from a lengthy study of US foreign policy during the CW, they are hidebound by the peculiarities of a superpower in the context of a bipolar international system and a stable domestic environment. This example does not fully exploit the analytical possibilities presented by investigating a wider pool of states, in particular, those involved in the processes of formation and transition. In these latter cases, the self-conscious use of foreign policy as a tool for nation-building and identity formation is patently evident, as is the necessity for interacting with the prevailing international power structures. His example more clearly illustrates the way that an examination of change in foreign policy exposes the foundational features of the international system.

Building on this perspective with respect to the foreign policy of transitional states, the act of making foreign policy becomes the process engaged in by the post-transitional state of socializing its actors around discourses of power within the international system, and establishing the material limits to and foundations of state-based action (i.e. foreign policy) within the international system. In addition, in the course of the transition process, the primordial questions of identity and citizenship are addressed, for example, What is the idea of the state? and What are the boundaries of the state and citizenship? Foreign policy is crucial for answering these questions and resolving the tenuousness of the initial response (or contrary responses from different groups within society) to an articulation of national identity based on hard materialist experience. The promulgation of foreign policy is what makes states; what defined South Africa's post-apartheid foreign policy fits within the broad framework of this understanding of the role of foreign policy in transitional states. South Africa's foreign policy represents the dual impulses – unilateralist idealist foreign policy and socialization to established practices and discourses of power – of the transformative agenda of a newly installed non-state actor.[46] Unilateralism under Mandela sought to challenge established international norms on sovereignty (Taiwan) and human rights (Nigeria and Indonesia), emerging out of the new social identity in post-apartheid South Africa, through a series of controversial foreign policy stances. Mbeki's 'embedded liberal idealism' represented both a compromise with the established international liberal order by adopting its economic policy prescriptions and, concurrently, a recognition that the possibilities of introducing new norms into the international and regional system would be more likely through active engagement in international and regional institutions. (South Africa's role in promulgating the New Partnership for Africa's Development and the formation of the African Union along lines that conformed to Pretoria's interests are the best expressions of this.)

Furthermore, the notion of the proximity of the foreign policy of a transitional state and its relationship to the social construction of national identity is especially evident in the South African case. 'South African-ness' emerged out of the turmoil of racially divisive politics, international isolation and revolutionary fervour, derived through the experience of formulating and implementing a new foreign policy for the post-apartheid state. The ANC's dual experience as a liberation movement and a civil rights campaign profoundly shaped the concerns of the Mandela government, while under Mbeki the 'two worlds' analysis of domestic politics, which reflected the economic divisions between blacks and whites, provided the impetus for South Africa's Africa policy and its 'developing south' orientation. For Mandela, making human rights the 'centrepiece' of post-apartheid foreign policy was a deliberate attempt to imbue the country's new foreign policy with the defining experience of black South Africans under apartheid, that is, denial of their basic human rights. For Mbeki, the enduring economic inequalities experienced by the majority of black South Africans reflected the inequalities between the countries in the developing south, especially in Africa, and the countries in the industrialized north. His foreign policy orientation towards Africa and the south was a conscious evocation of this fundamental experience as well as an echo of the solidarity politics of the revolutionary period. It is in this way, echoing the links made by Campbell between the constant reproduction of foreign policy and the formative shaping and re-assertion of national identity, that foreign policy can be seen as crucial to the nation building process.

Conclusion

This examination of the under-researched phenomenon of change in foreign policy provides both an overview of the existing contributions to the FPA literature on that topic and an integration of the work on political regimes, transitions and revolutions, which has a strong bearing on the topic, but has remained outside the purview of classical FPA. These bodies of literature may be used by FPA to examine analytically what to expect in terms of foreign policy when states go through change. Our reflections on what foreign policy change might entail for clustered and quasi-states suggests how students of FPA might be able to link the conceptual and analytical strands of the literature on change we examined. The cobbling together of this material gives a better sense than the established and limited FPA work would suggest of the place of change in the conduct of individuals and the shaping of decision-making processes, and beyond that, of the structural implications of change and its impact on foreign policy. Finally, we have put forward a set of propositions based on constructivism and foreign policy which we believe provides a more cogent interpretation of the relationship and also underlines the consequential nature of foreign policy in the formative concerns of national identity construction.

8 Conclusion
New directions in foreign policy analysis

A key rationale behind this book has been our desire to provide the basis for a contemporary critical assessment of FPA, which engages with developments within IR. This has involved a re-examination of premises that have been at the centre of FPA and for the most part remained largely unquestioned. In our view, one of the most consequential oversights is the absence of a theory of the state in FPA, with the corollary of FPA's primary focus on decision making and the specific epistemological emphases it has given to that process. This in turn has been exacerbated by FPA scholars' failure to adequately engage with critical intellectual developments in IR over the last two decades. This is strongly reflected in the exclusion of the debate on globalization from FPA and the inadequate engagement with constructivism, with special reference to foreign policy change. In the sections that follow, we offer for consideration some critical observations and analyses of the central challenges facing FPA flowing from our assessments of the field today as well as possible areas for future development.

FPA and decision making

Foreign policy decision making has been and remains at the core of the 'FPA project' and its enduring contribution to IR. The tilting effect generated by the 'decision-making turn' (as one might call it retrospectively) on realism and its grip on the study of IR are mainstreamed now within the discipline. On closer examination, however, the seminal contribution of FPA on decision making and the continued focus on that aspect of the foreign policy process strikes one as flawed and imbalanced. Foreign policy decision-making theory is predicated on a systems approach. It assumes that there is a feedback loop of information from the 'external environment' to policy makers, allowing for readjustment and innovation. Yet the decision-making approach still suffers from some significant shortcoming. Decisions are depicted as *sui generis*, outside of history and its cycles, without reference to previous decisions nor the accompanying interpretations by decision makers. One expression of this is the dilemma facing rationalists in explaining the formation of preferences which are uncritically assigned motivation primacy but are notoriously difficult to square with empirical studies of actual decisions and the perspectives of those involved. As we saw in Chapter 2, the inconvenient truth of misperception, bias and other equivalent 'pathologies' that formed the critique of foreign policy decision making in FPA nonetheless could not bring scholars to wrestle themselves away from the underlying systems theory framework. As such the decision-making formulation retains an unrecognized commitment to this rationalist model and its narrow application to the decision-making unit, which continues to hold an impact on analyses of the decision-making process. Beyond these issues, the role of foreign policy implementation as a neglected component of the foreign policy equation too remains barely examined especially with respect to varieties of actors, their articulation of the boundaries of foreign policy within the confines of the states and how the foreign policy decision making process operates under these circumstances. Agents on the ground, their parochial interpretation of national foreign policy directives and the form these take when translated into local actions is a feature of the feedback loop that arguably is as consequential a part of the decision making as the original formulation. Studies of other types of sub-national foreign policy actors such as provinces remain few and far between as well, rendering the capacity of FPA to provide an interpretation of the globalizing international system far less credible. Furthermore, it contributes to a perception that FPA is unable to grasp and integrate globalization and account for its attendant impact on the contemporary international politics. By elucidating the pertinence of recent debates in IR to FPA the remainder of the chapter seeks to broaden the narrow focus FPA has placed on the decision-making unit.

FPA and broader debates in IR

Globalization theory

Since its inception FPA has engaged with several literatures, for example, public choice theory, political psychology, cognitive theory. Within the discipline of IR, FPA has been part of an ongoing dialogue with realism and, more recently, has developed links with constructivism.

In our three critiques of classical FPA new bodies of literature have emerged as pertinent to the study of foreign policy. This theoretical eclecticism has been a constant feature of FPA scholarship over the years. To our mind it is one of the strengths of its analytical approach and should continue to be encouraged. In this context, Chapter 6 suggests a potential link between FPA and globalization theory, based upon FPA engaging with what we have termed the mutually constitutive thesis of globalization. This thesis is useful in FPA because it strikes a balance between the causal roles it ascribes to military-political forces and economic-social-technological forces in its conception of globalization, its origins and its impact. Corresponding with this view, we identified the rise of *contemporary* globalization during the CW. In this period there was an expansion of social relations to the global scale, accompanied by a change in the international political structure of social relations. From this vantage point, the intersection between FPA and globalization theory is seen as mutually beneficial. Employing FPA in the study of globalization enhances our understanding of the process in a number of ways. We have expressed the view that foreign policy is not extinguished by globalization. In fact, it would appear that in a more interconnected world, but still divided by political borders, foreign policy remains one of the key sites for political action that is available to states. Thus, one of the contributions of FPA to enhancing our understanding of globalization is to explain how and to what extent foreign policy is used by states to seize the opportunities and to meet the challenges imposed by globalization.

Another added value of FPA is its ability to elucidate the way that foreign policy impacts on the interface between international politics and globalization. We have argued in Chapter 6 that the relationship between international politics and globalization is dialectic, simultaneously producing globalizing and fragmenting effects. However, as the example of the CW suggests, at certain historical junctures globalization and international politics can be mutually constitutive. FPA, with its conception of foreign policy as a boundary activity, on the cusp between the domestic and external spheres, is ideally placed to explore this dialectic relationship further.

Finally, the central role ascribed to foreign policy of shaping the processes of globalization affords a greater place for human agency in the design of globalization than globalization theory would concede. Chapter 6 shows that the liberal, capitalist and democratic imprint of contemporary globalization is linked to the design of the global cluster. This insight suggests that globalization is less accidental and out of control than the transformationalist and hyperglobalist theses would suggest. Indeed the 'return of the state' in the aftermath of the global financial crisis of 2008–9, both in terms of its effective nationalization of the ailing financial sectors in the industrialized north and the mercantilist conduct of emerging powers within the international system, is an indication of the limited and contingent nature of these theoretical approaches. It also means that the imperfections that FPA identifies in the process of decision making and implementation – cognitive biases, group thinking and bureaucratic politics – may play a role in the production and reproduction of globalization. The FPA literature on these issues of decision making would inform further development of this research agenda.

An encounter between FPA and the mutually constitutive thesis would contribute not only to our understanding of the role foreign policy plays in globalization, but would have implications for the concepts we use to explain foreign policy decision making and implementation in these conditions. Although FPA challenges some of the key premises in realism, it endorses (if unwittingly) one key assumption: that the state is a territorially bounded entity. In the context of the insights from the mutually constitutive thesis, this assumption might need to be revisited although FPA concedes that the boundary between the domestic and the external environments is porous. However, this alone is not sufficient to capture the changing conditions of statehood in the context of globalization. Thus, if as we have argued a concurrent set of changes – the elimination of borders of violence, the pooling of sovereignty and authority, and the creation of a global state layer of institutions – is underway, then this will have implications for the core concepts of FPA. More specifically, decision making, bureaucratic politics, the societal and statist determinants of foreign policy must become more embedded in global networks than is allowed for in the contemporary frameworks employed by FPA. By engaging with the mutually constitutive thesis of globalization FPA scholars should be better placed to examine the implications of globalization for the key concepts employed in FPA.

Historical sociology

Chapter 5 examined three tensions generated by the lack within FPA of a conception of the state. The result is threefold. First, foreign policy analysts draw on a set of assumptions about states without explicitly recognizing them. This drives the thinking of the foreign policy analyst in ways that are not overtly recognized. Second, foreign policy is rendered a mere extension of foreign policy determinants – individual, bureaucratic, societal or external – making it difficult if not impossible to account for foreign policy as a distinct site of action. Third, since FPA includes investigation of foreign policy this is a recognition that the latter is relatively autonomous of society and of external forces, but in the absence of a conception of the state FPA is not able to account for that autonomy.

Chapter 5 addresses these epistemological, ontological and conceptual tensions by analytically reconciling FPA and historical sociology, with reference to the literature on the state. From this literature we derived conceptions of the institutional state, the quasi-state and the clustered state, definitions that are based on the level of material statehood exhibited by each type. Chapter 5 shows that using these conceptions of the state has concrete implications for the assumptions informing FPA in relation to the use of foreign policy tools, the source of state autonomy and the relationship between the state and the external environment, allowing us to address the three tensions identified above. Chapter 7 offered reflections on how these state types and foreign policy change might be connected.

Yet in our view, the analytical reconciliation between historical sociology and FPA can make a contribution that goes beyond addressing the tensions identified above. Empirically, as Halliday's work on the Middle East referred to in Chapter 5 shows, this encounter has much to offer. For example, it is able to capture long-term changes affecting foreign policy, and the interlinkages between the three levels of analysis underpinning international politics. This operationalizes one of the key criticisms of FPA of the realist tradition in IR, that foreign policy decision making, implementation and, therefore, outcomes, are not shaped only by inter-state relations, but are defined by the dynamics among multiple levels of activity – domestic, state, international, global.

Another research direction relates to the methodological opportunities that derive from an analytical reconciliation between FPA and historical sociology. Although FPA challenges realism on many levels, its early accounts too easily accepted the realist approach of IR as a normal science. As noted earlier more recent approaches favour maintaining FPA as a middle-range theory and in this context we believe historical sociology has much to offer in terms of providing FPA with a sound ontological grounding. In Chapter 6 we demonstrate the utility of a neo-Weberian ontology for determining, conceptually and analytically, the roles that foreign policy might play in the context of globalization. In not seeking to establish ontological primacy, a neo-Weberian approach is suited to FPA in light of the latter's emphasis on elucidating other complex causal relationships. For example, whether regional positioning generates a particular foreign policy; the extent to which socio-economic/military-political structures generate impacts propelling a particular foreign policy. In examining these questions we are not advocating a return to geo-politics, dependency theories or applying variants of neo-realism to FPA. Instead, we are calling for comparative analytical-historical studies exploring these issues, with the aim of highlighting the conditions under which we might expect recurrences in foreign policy decision making, implementation and behaviour.

A third contribution concerns the US bias within FPA. As we saw in Chapters 2 and 3 the modelling of foreign policy decision making by FPA scholars, its core insights and key principles are derivative of the US foreign policy system and experience. These have been, admittedly, applied out to a variety of non-US cases over the years – and with greater frequency today than a decade ago. However, the categories and epistemological tools employed to study 'non-US' or 'non-Western' foreign policy remain bounded by these origins. Korany's critical commentary on the absence of any serious effort to assess foreign policy decision making in the 'Third World' in its own terms has left FPA scholars in the position of too often misapplying these culturally specific approaches to the task of interpreting decision making in distant settings with the expected (failed) outcomes.[1] In proposing a tripartite state typology – institutional, clustered and quasi – we provide FPA with an opening to locate decision-making structures within contexts that do not derive from the structure underpinning the state in the case of the US.

Finally, in our view, an analytical reconciliation between FPA and historical sociology would require a more serious consideration of historicity in FPA. We do not refer here to the use of history or of reference to history, in which respects FPA is well versed. Rather, we refer to the tendency FPA shares with other approaches in IR to assume the texture of IR to be timeless. However, historical sociologists studying IR, especially Little and Buzan, provide evidence that the texture of IR is anything but timeless. International societies *do* change. Norms are contingent and reinterpreted by state and non-state actors over time. Foreign policy decision making is a process that evolves and responds to changing conditions within the halls of policy and the wider society. FPA should recognize as formative these conditions of change affecting the mutually constitutive relationship between foreign policy and international politics.[2] We hope that in opening up the possibility of an encounter between FPA and historical sociology, we are promoting further developments in this direction.

Constructivism

Our efforts to critically examine FPA and some of its underlying features not only highlight the constructed characteristics of sovereignty but the very process of formulating (and ultimately implementing) a state's foreign policy. Constructivism, still in the main overlooked by FPA scholars,[3] provides a coherent set of insights and analyses of practice which cohere well with core interests of FPA scholarship. Indeed, as aleady mentioned in Chapter 7, some of the primal insights and critiques of FPA reflected a constructivist impulse decades before constructivism itself was formally introduced as an innovative challenge to the prevailing realist paradigm.

This is most evident in our examination of foreign policy and transitional states where ideational factors translated into foreign policy prescriptions and come into direct contact with the structural dimensions of the international system. A logic of appropriateness is clearly the driving force in the shaping foreign policy choice by transitional states. The dynamic interaction that follows between the post-authoritarian foreign policy and the norms, regimes and institutions that undergird the international system establishes parameters within which the transitional state can act. They challenge underlying assumptions, provide alternative sources (and socially more consonant forms) of legitimacy, and introduce new meaning to norms, rules and institutions that govern the international system.

But constructivism can be more readily brought into other aspects of FPA. For instance, Chapter 3 pointed to Weldes's constructivist critique of the theory of bureaucratic politics. Revisiting the BPM from a critical constructivist vantage point, Weldes's work provides a powerful challenge of the key notions underlying Allison and his followers' work: interests, power, rationality. Another case in point is the literature on 'learning' in foreign policy. It is focused on the policy makers at the top but it is evident that a closer reading of foreign policy implementation would undoubtedly highlight the degree to which such learning takes place at other levels within the structures of foreign policy making. Moreover, the interaction between states and non-state actors in devising or altering regimes – be they in the context of climate change, security or elsewhere – would benefit from a constructivist interpretation of foreign policy which captures the changing yet decisive role of the state in this process. This would, as underscored in our work on globalization and foreign policy, contribute to a better recognition of the agency involved in the globalization process.

At the same time, it is important to keep in mind and interrogate some 'hidden' assumptions featured in constructivist accounts of change which have an impact of our understanding of foreign policy. Underlying much of constructivism's focus on norms are abiding liberal notions of progress and modernity and their purported inevitable if not seamless march into the future. Historical sociology's reading of state formation tells us that the institutional forms that emerge in the wake of – and concurrent with – great societal and economic change differ not only in relation to the societies involved but contingencies of all sorts produce varied outcomes. Foreign policy change, linked intimately of course to the same forces, exhibits the same diversity of experiences and outcomes and any assumptions which are predicated on expectations of ideologically convergent foreign policies by states undergoing consequential change are misguided at best. From the rise of illiberal democracies to the rapid spread of the Salafist ideology through the internet, evidence of disturbing counters-trends to teleological readings of the present (and future) abound. As Wang Jisi warns us with respect to China's gradualist development of a grand strategy, 'these developments are unfolding haltingly and are by no means irreversible'.[4]

Neo-classical realism

Of all the theoretical developments emerging from IR in the last decade, perhaps the most surprising is the revitalization of realism in the form of what its proponents call neo-classical realism. Crucial to the formulation of this novel branch of realism is a deliberate embracing of aspects of unit-level analysis – bringing its proponents directly into the realm of 'foreign policy', the very area which Waltz consciously steered away from in his influential structuralist rendering of realism. Neoclassical realism's integration of 'intervening variables' such as the role of perception, the role of leadership and domestic structures found within particular state actors as an explanatory source for diversity of outcomes in international politics brings these three crucial FPA insights into the realist theoretical paradigm. By directly folding in ideas that had always implicitly tied to notions of perception such as states' concerns with relative power and perceptions of threat, neo-classical realists are able to account for the subjective understandings of events and differing foreign policy choices that routinely characterized state action. The inclusion of leadership as a crucial variable in mobilizing the material resources in a given state reasserts the agency of individuals and the place of contingencies in state action.

And, recognizing the diversity of domestic institutional structures and their concomitant impact on formative foreign policy capacity and actual implementation captures in elementary form the means by which structural dimensions at the unit-level come into play in shaping state action.

Not all the innovations currently presented by neo-classical realists and others in IR, however, draw out in full the implications of some of the work in FPA. For instance going beyond the mere recognition of domestic structure as significant by neo-classical realists to a more developed understanding of the actual relationship between political regime type and its institutional manifestations with respect to civil-military ties would open up a more nuanced sense of the sources of threat perception and its consequences for state conduct. Perceptions of risk adversity in foreign policy on the part of a given regime could, one imagines, be more strongly correlated to the nature of civil-military ties than the current ideologically bounded (and flawed) consideration of the consequences of regime type in producing systemic-level peace. Continuing to develop neo-classical realism's interest in the role of leadership in relation to societal forces, without detouring too much into decision-making processes, could be strengthened by examining the work on public opinion, the media and foreign policy. Revisiting the work on hierarchies of state power – in particular the existing literature on middle powers which anticipates many of NCR's insights in linking perceptions of power and identity, leadership/followership, and resource mobilisation to foreign policy – would enrich an approach that still devotes too much of its focus to 'great powers.' Though neo-classical realists remain wedded to the international system as an unassailable independent variable, the scope for developing greater theoretical depth through careful 'borrowing' from FPA without sacrificing this principle is wide.

From 'normal science' to empirics?

Throughout the book FPA has been shown to straddle two key methodological approaches. On the one hand, and especially in the early years, FPA aimed at beating realism on its positivist home ground. In Chapter 2 we show how a behaviourist approach and cognition theory were used to develop a workable framework that captured the beliefs of a leader in a systemic way with the aim of producing predictions about foreign policy decision making. These were subsequently folded into a broader comparative foreign policy project that attempted to devise a generalizable theory through the application of quantitative techniques. Chapter 3 describes how Allison and colleagues tried to develop the BPM into a normal science and Chapter 7 notes the attempts to link state type, region and foreign policy change.

Recent approaches in FPA question the utility of these attempts and have challenged the route of FPA as a normal science. A number of the accounts explored in this book, from Minz's poliheuristic approach to decision making, to Welch's revisionist take on bureaucratic politics, to work linking foreign policy change to state type set a more modest agenda for FPA: that of devising a conceptual and analytical framework that provides the tools for foreign policy analysts to study the empirical phenomena related to foreign policy. These approaches reinforce FPA's orientation as a middle-range theory. This allows FPA to uncover a diversity of elements that constitute foreign policy and to account for them in conceptual and analytical terms within the middle ground between IR as normal science and research driven purely by empirics.

Our intervention, calling for FPA to explore the themes of change, globalization and the state, reinforces this view. We have not sought to develop parsimonious accounts that will provide FPA with the tools to predict foreign policy outcomes in the context of change, globalization and how the autonomy of the state flows to foreign policy. Rather, our schema encourages FPA scholars to use our proposed formulation as a roadmap providing conceptual and analytical frameworks to explore these three themes. Hence, our tripartite conception of the state – clustered, institutionalist, quasi – to study the impact of the state on foreign policy. In a similar vein we have suggested the utility of employing a neo-Weberian ontology to study the role of foreign policy in the context of globalization.

Positioning FPA as a middle-range theory, of course, exacts a price from FPA in terms of its ability to make general claims about the nature of foreign policy (and through that, international politics). However, in our view, this limitation is justified because of the analytical clarity it confers to the role played by what we call *axial factors* in foreign policy. Axial factors are an ontological part of foreign policy. They act like a wheel axle to propel foreign policy in different directions. Certain of the elements explored in this book qualify as axial factors – decision makers, bureaucracies, societal actors, the state. In its orientation as a middle-range theory, FPA seems well placed to examine the interlinkages between the axial elements of foreign policy decision making, foreign policy implementation, and foreign policy behaviour in a cross national context. In the end, scholars studying foreign policy have the benefit of a rich tradition that provides a solid foundation for achieving a better understanding of international politics. Informed by the cross-fertilization we have proposed with other debates in IR, suggested in this book, we hope that we have presented new avenues and directions that FPA might pursue in its ongoing endeavour to account for the complex subject matter of foreign policy.

Notes

1 Foreign policy analysis – an overview

1 J. David Singer, 'The level-of-analysis problem in international relations', *World Politics*, 1961, vol. 14, no. 1, pp. 77–92.
2 For a discussion in the context of FPA see Walter Carlsnaes, 'The agency-structure problem in foreign policy analysis', *International Studies Quarterly*, 1992, vol. 36, no. 3, pp. 245–70.
3 Richard Snyder, Henry W. Bruck and Burton Sapin, 'Decision making as an approach to the study of international politics', in Richard Snyder, Henry W. Bruck and Burton Sapin (eds) *Foreign Policy Decision Making: An Approach to International Politics*, New York: Free Press/Macmillan, 1962, p. 177. For instance see section on motivation, perception and frames of reference in Snyder et al., op. cit., pp. 136–60.
4 David Patrick Houghton, 'Reinvigorating the study of foreign policy decision making: Toward a constructivist approach', *Foreign Policy Analysis*, 2007, vol. 3, no. 1, pp. 24–45.
5 The emphasis on borrowing from other fields featured in the seminal work on FPA by Snyder et al., op. cit. p. 27: 'Thus far, we have not effectively linked Area Studies, Comparative Government, Public Administration, Political Theory, and Political Parties, to say nothing of History, Philosophy and the Social Sciences, to (the study of) International Politics'.
6 See Hans Morgenthau, *Politics Among Nations*, New York: Knopf, 1948.
7 See Snyder et al., op. cit.; James Rosenau, 'Pre-theories and theories of foreign policy', in Robert B. Farrell (ed.) *Approaches in Comparative and International Politics*, Evanston, IL: Northwestern University Press, 1966; For an updating of the argument, see also James Rosenau, 'A pre-theory revisited: World politics in an era of cascading interdependence', *International Studies Quarterly*, 1984, vol. 28, no. 3, pp. 245–305.
8 Kenneth Boulding, *The Image: Knowledge in Life and Society*, Ann Arbor, MI: Arbor Paperbacks, 1956.
9 Graham T. Allison and Morton H. Halperin, 'Bureaucratic politics: A paradigm and some policy implications', *World Politics*, 1972, vol. 24, pp. 40–79.
10 See, e.g., Lloyd Jensen, *Explaining Foreign Policy*, Englewood Cliffs, NJ: Prentice Hall, 1982, pp. 199–231.
11 Haral Muller and Thomas Risse-Kappen, 'From the outside in and from the inside out', in David Skidmore and Valerie M. Hudson, *The Limits of*

State Autonomy, Boulder, CO: Westview Press, 1993, p. 33. See also Christopher Hill, 'What is left of the domestic?' in Michi Ebata (ed.), *Confronting the Political in International Relations,* London: Macmillan, 2000, pp. 159–65 especially.

12 Roy E. Jones, *Principles of Foreign Policy – The Civil State in its World Setting,* Oxford: Martin Robertson, 1979, pp. 88–104. Muller and Risse-Kappen, op. cit., pp. 38–47. See also Miroslav Ninic, *Democracy and Foreign Policy: The Fallacy of Political Realism,* New York: Columbia University Press, 1992; Christopher Hill, *The Changing Politics of Foreign Policy,* Basingstoke: Palgrave, 2003, pp. 235–40; Thomas Risse-Kappen, 'Democratic peace – warlike democracies? A social constructivist interpretation of the liberal argument', *European Journal of International Relations,* 1995, vol. 1, no. 4, pp. 491–517; Randolf J. Rummel, 'Democracies are less warlike than other regimes', *European Journal of International Relations,* 1995, vol. 1, no. 4, pp. 649–64; Bruce M. Russet, *Grasping the Democratic Peace: Principles for a Post-Cold War World,* Princeton, NJ: Princeton University Press, 1993.

13 Hill, *The Changing Politics of Foreign Policy,* p. 193.

14 The literature on the external environment as a pluralist environment has focused on TNAs and developed in two stages. For the first transnational debate see, amongst others, Edward L. Morse, 'Modernization and the transformation of foreign policies: Modernization, interdependence and externalization', *World Politics,* 1970, vol. 22, no. 3, pp. 371–92; Joseph S. Nye and Robert O. Keohane (eds) *Transnational Relations and World Politics,* Cambridge, MA: Harvard University Press, 1970; Samuel Huntington, 'Transnational organizations in world politics', *World Politics,* 1973, vol. 25, no. 3, pp. 333–68; Richard W. Mansbach, Yale H. Ferguson and Donald E. Lampert, *The Web of World Politics: Non-State Actors in the Global System,* London: Prentice Hall, 1976. For a good summary of the transition from the first to the second waves of the literature on TNAs see Thomas Risse-Kappen (ed.) *Bringing Transnational Relations Back In: Non-State Actors, Domestic Structures, and International Institutions,* Cambridge: Cambridge University Press, 1995; Daphner Josselin and William Wallace (eds) *Non-State Actors in World Politics,* London: Palgrave, 2001, especially pp. 12–13; Hill, *The Changing Politics of Foreign Policy,* especially chapter on Transnational formulations.

15 Robert Putnam, 'Diplomacy and domestic politics: The logic of two-level games', *International Organization,* 1988, vol. 42, no. 3, pp. 427–60. Putnam's concept of two-level games has been applied in several studies. See, amongst others, Howard. P. Lehman and Jennifer L. Mckoy, 'The dynamics of the two-level bargaining game: The 1988 Brazilian debt negotiations', *World Politics,* 1992, vol. 44, no. 2, pp. 600–44; Keisuke Iieda, 'When and how do domestic constraints matter? Two-level games with uncertainty', *Journal of Conflict Resolution,* 1993, vol. 37, no. 2, pp. 403–26; Peter B. Evans, Harold K. Jacobson and Robert D. Putnam (eds) *Double-Edged Diplomacy,* Berkeley: University of California Press, 1993. Putnam's account also inspired broader theoretical works on the connection between the domestic and international see James A. Caporaso, 'Across the great divide: Integrating comparative and international politics', *International Study Quarterly,* 1997, vol. 41, no. 4, pp. 563–91.

16 Joe Hagan, 'Domestic political explanations in the analysis of foreign policy', in Laura Neack, Jeanne Hey and Patrick Haney (eds) *Foreign Policy Analysis: Continuity and Change in its Second Generation*, Englewood Cliffs, NJ: Prentice Hall, 1995, p. 117.

17 Hill, *The Changing Politics of Foreign Policy*, p. 87.

18 David Held, Anthony G. McGrew, David Goldblat and Jonathan Perraton, *Global Transformations: Politics, Economics, Culture*, Cambridge: Polity Press, 1999.

19 On the significance of Held et al.'s work in the context of GT see Joseph S. Nye and Robert O. Keohane, 'Globalization: What's new? What's not? (And so what?)', *Foreign Policy*, 2000, vol. 118, no. 1, p. 119. Other transformationalist works include Anthony Giddens, *The Consequences of Modernity*, Cambridge: Polity Press, 1991; Anthony Giddens, *Runaway World*, London: Profile Books, 1999; James N. Rosenau, *Along the Domestic–Foreign Frontier: Exploring Governance in a Turbulent World*, Cambridge: Cambridge University Press, 1997; Jan Aart Scholte, *Globalization: A Critical Introduction*, Basingstoke: Palgrave Macmillan, 2005.

20 For the tenets of GT see Justin Rosenberg, 'Globalisation theory: A post mortem', *International Politics*, 2005, vol. 42, no. 1, p. 4.

21 Rosenberg, 'Globalisation theory: A post mortem', p. 2.

22 See Anna Leander, '"Globalisation theory": Feeble ... and hijacked', *International Political Sociology*, 2009, vol. 3, pp. 109–12.

23 Albert, e.g. argues that GT's fortunes lie in Luhmanian theorizing. See Mathias Albert, '"Globalisation theory" Yesterday's fad or more lively than ever?', *International Political Sociology*, 2007, vol. 2, pp. 165–82. Robertson sees theorizing around global consciousness and connectivity as promising avenues for GT. Roland Robertson, 'Differentiational reductionism and the missing link in Albert's approach to globalisation theory', *International Political Sociology*, 2009, vol. 3, pp. 119–22; David Held and Anthony McGrew, *Globalisation Theory: Approaches and Controversies*, Cambridge: Polity Press, 2007.

24 An examination of the index entries in the following works reveals the absence of 'foreign policy'. See, e.g., Held et al., op. cit., *Global Transformations*; David Held and Anthony McGrew (eds) *The Global Transformations Reader*, Cambridge: Polity Press, 2003; Jan Aart Scholte, *Globalization: A Critical Introduction*, Basingstoke: Palgrave Macmillan, 2005; Jan Aart Scholte and Ronald Robertson, *Encyclopedia of Globalisation*, New York: Routledge, 2007. See also recent forums on GT in *International Politics*, vol. 42, no. 3, 2005, pp. 364–99 and *International Political Sociology*, vol. 31, no. 1, 2009, pp. 109–28.

25 E.g. Steve Smith, Amelia Hadfield and Tim Dunne, *Foreign Policy: Theories, Actors, Cases*, Oxford: Oxford University Press, 2008; Valerie M. Hudson, *Foreign Policy Analysis: Classic and Contemporary Theory*, Lanham, MD: Rowman & Littlefield, 2007.

26 Hill, *The Changing Politics of Foreign Policy*, pp. 189–93.

27 Mark Webber and Michael Smith (eds) *Foreign Policy in a Transformed World*, Harlow: Prentice Hall, 2002.

28 David Welch, *Painful Choices: A Theory of Foreign Policy Change*, Princeton, NJ: Princeton University Press, 2005.

29 See, e.g., the work on Gorbechev, such as Janice Stein, 'Political learning by doing: Gorbachev as uncommitted thinker and motivated learner', *International Organization*, 1994, vol. 48, no. 2, pp. 155–83.

30 Brian Ripley, 'Cognition, culture and bureaucratic politics' in Laura Neack, Jeanne Hey and Patrick Haney (eds) *Foreign Policy Analysis: Continuity and Change in its Second Generation*, Englewood Cliffs, NJ: Prentice Hall, 1995.

31 Michael Barnett, 'Culture, strategy and foreign policy change: Israel's road to Oslo', *European Journal of International Relations*, 1999, vol. 5, no. 1, pp. 5–36.

32 Alison Stanger, 'Democratization and the international system', in Miles Kahler (ed.) *Liberalization and Foreign Policy*, New York: Columbia University Press, 1997.

2 Foreign policy decision making

1 Margot Light, 'Foreign policy analysis', in A.J.R. Groom and Margot Light (eds) *Contemporary International Relations: A Guide to Theory*, London: Pinter, 1994, pp. 93–108; Laura Neack, Jeanne Hey and Patrick Haney, 'Generational change in foreign policy analysis', in Laura Neack, Jeanne Hey and Patrick Haney (eds) *Foreign Policy Analysis: Continuity and Change in its Second Generation*, Englewood Cliffs, NJ: Prentice Hall, 1995, pp. 5–8. A selection of the literature embracing the rationalist approach to foreign policy includes works such as Thomas Schelling, *The Strategy of Conflict*, Cambridge, MA: Harvard University Press, 1960; Leon Sigal, 'The rational policy model and the Formosa Straits crisis', *International Studies Quarterly*, 1970, vol. 14, no. 2, pp. 121–56; Robert Putnam, 'Diplomacy and domestic politics: The logic of two-level games', *International Organization*, 1988, vol. 42; George Tsebelis, *Nested Games: Rational Choice in Comparative Politics*, Berkeley: University of California Press, 1990; Peter Evans, Harold Jacobson and Robert Putnam (eds) *Double-Edged Diplomacy: International Bargaining and Domestic Politics*, Berkeley: University of California Press, 1993; Helen Milner, *Interests, Institutions and Information: Domestic Politics and International Relations*, Princeton, NJ: Princeton University Press, 1997.

2 See formative texts such as Richard Snyder, H.W. Bruck and Burton Sapin, *Foreign Policy Decision-Making: An Approach to the Study of International Politics*, New York: Macmillan, 1962; and Harold Sprout and Margaret Sprout, *Man–Milieu Relationship Hypotheses in the Context of International Politics*, Princeton, NJ: Princeton University Press, 1956.

3 James Rosenau, 'Pre-theories and theories and foreign policy', in R.B. Farrell (ed.) *Approaches to Comparative and International Politics*, Evanston, IL: Northwestern University Press, 1966; Rosenau offers a trenchant critique of this seminal article in later years; see James Rosenau, 'A pre-theory revisited: World politics in an era of cascading interdependence', *International Studies Quarterly*, 1984, vol. 38, pp. 245–305.

4 Gary Snyder and Paul Diesing, *Conflict Among Nations: Bargaining, Decision Making and System Structure in International Crises*, Princeton, NJ: Princeton University Press, 1977.

5 Robert Powell, *Nuclear Deterrence Theory*, New York: Cambridge University Press, 1990.

6 Schelling, op. cit.; see also Kathleen Archibald (ed.) *Strategic Interaction and Conflict,* Berkeley: University of California Press, 1966.

7 Robert Putnam, op. cit.

8 Gilat Levy and Ronny Razin, 'It takes two: An explanation for the democratic peace', *Journal of the European Economic Association,* 2004, vol. 2, no. 2, pp. 1–29.

9 Robert Jervis, *Perception and Misperception in International Politics,* Princeton, NJ: Princeton University Press, 1976. See also Robert Jervis, 'Hypotheses on misperception', *World Politics,* 1968, vol. 20, no. 3, pp. 454–79.

10 Peter Katzenstein, 'International relations and domestic structures: Foreign economic policies of advanced industrial states', *International Organization,* 1976, vol. 30, no. 1, pp. 1–45.

11 Ahmer Tarar, 'International bargaining with two-sided domestic constraints', *Journal of Conflict Resolution,* 2001, vol. 45, no. 3, pp. 320–2; see also Tsebelis, op. cit.

12 Harold Sprout and Margaret Sprout, op. cit.

13 Snyder et al., op. cit.

14 Snyder et al., op. cit., p. 65.

15 Valeria Hudson, 'Foreign policy analysis: Actor-specific theory and the ground of international relations', *Foreign Policy Analysis,* 2005, vol. 1, no. 1, p. 30.

16 Janice G. Stein, 'Foreign policy decision making: Rational, psychological and neurological models', in Steven Smith, Amelia Hadfield and Timothy Dunne (eds) *Foreign Policy: Theories, Actors, Cases,* Oxford: Oxford University Press, 2008, pp. 104–9.

17 Robert Jervis, op. cit., pp. 217–79.

18 Ole Holsti, 'Foreign policy formation viewed cognitively', in Robert Axelrod (ed.) *Structure of Decision: The Cognitive Maps of Political Elites,* Princeton, NJ: Princeton University Press, 1976; Ole Holsti, 'The belief system and national images: A case study', *Journal of Conflict Resolution,* 1962, vol. 6, no. 3, pp. 244–52.

19 Kenneth Boulding, 'National images and international systems' *Journal of Conflict Resolution,* 1959, vol. 3, no. 2, pp. 120–31.

20 Susan Fiske and Shelley Taylor, *Social Cognition,* New York: McGraw-Hill, 1984, pp. 72–99.

21 Robert Jervis, op. cit., pp. 117–19.

22 Leon Festinger, cited in Christopher Hill, *The Changing Politics of Foreign Policy,* Basingstoke: Palgrave, 2003, p. 114.

23 Jerel Rosati, 'A cognitive guide to the study of foreign policy', in Laura Neack, Jeanne Hey and Patrick Haney (eds), op. cit., pp. 63–4.

24 Alexander George, 'The "Operational Code": A neglected approach to the study of political leaders and decision-making', *International Studies Quarterly,* 1969, vol. 13, no. 2, pp. 190–222.

25 Robert Axelrod, op. cit.

26 Herbert Simon, cited in Christopher Hill, *The Changing Politics of Foreign Policy,* Basingstoke: Palgrave, 2003, p. 103.

27 For a discussion on this point see Richard Ned Lebow, 'The Cuban missile crisis: Reading the lessons correctly', *Political Studies Quarterly,* vol. 98, no. 3, 1983, pp. 431–58.

28 Barton Bernstein, 'The Cuban missile crisis: Trading the Jupiters in Turkey?' *Political Science Quarterly*, 1980, vol. 95, no. 1, pp. 97–125.

29 Stephen Dyson, 'Personality and foreign policy: Tony Blair's Iraq decision', *Foreign Policy Analysis*, 2006, vol. 2, no. 3, pp. 289–306.

30 See, for example, Graham Shepard, 'Personality effects on American foreign policy, 1969–84: A second test of interpersonal generalization theory', *International Studies Quarterly*, 1988, vol. 32, no. 1, pp. 91–123.

31 Irving Janis and Leon Mann, *Decision Making*, New York: Free Press, 1977.

32 Jonathan Renshon and Stanley Renshon, 'Theory and practice of foreign policy decision making', *Political Psychology*, 2008, vol. 29, no. 4, pp. 509–36.

33 David G. Winter, 'Personality and foreign policy: Historical overview of research', in Eric Singer and Valerie Hudson (eds) *Political Psychology and Foreign Policy*, Boulder, CO: Westview, 1992, p. 79.

34 Cynthia Orbovich and Richard Molnar, 'Modeling foreign policy advisory processes', in Eric Singer and Valerie Hudson (eds) *Political Psychology and Foreign Policy*, Boulder, CO: Westview, 1992, p. 202.

35 Jonathan Renshon and Stanley Renshon, op. cit.

36 Yuen Foong Khong, 'Neoconservatism and the domestic sources of American foreign policy: The role of ideas in Operation Iraqi Freedom', in Smith et al., op. cit., pp. 261–2.

37 Irving Janis, *Groupthink: Psychological Studies of Policy Decisions and Fiascos*, Boston, MA: Houghton Mifflin, 1982.

38 Alexander George, 'The case for multiple advocacy in making foreign policy', *American Political Science Review*, 1972, vol. 66, no.3, pp. 731–85.

39 Paul 't Hart, Eric Stern and and Bengt Sundelius *Beyond Groupthink: Political Group Dynamics and Foreign Policy-making*, Ann Arbor, MI: University of Michigan Press, 1997.

40 Ole Holsti, 'The operational code approach to the study of political leaders: John Foster Dulles' philosophical and instrumental beliefs', *Canadian Journal of Political Science*, 1970, vol. 3, no. 1, p. 27.

41 Martin Hollis and Steve Smith, 'Roles and reasons in foreign policy decision making', *British Journal of Political Science*, 1986, vol. 16, no. 3, pp. 269–86.

42 David Houghton, 'Reinvigorating the study of foreign policy decision making: Towards a constructivist approach', *Foreign Policy Analysis*, 2007, vol. 3, vol. 1, pp. 24–45.

43 Elisabetta Brighi and Christopher Hill, 'Implementation and behaviour', in Smith et al., op. cit., pp. 117–36.

44 Charles E. Lindblom, 'The science of muddling through', *Public Administration Review*, 1959, vol. 19, no. 2, pp. 79–88.

45 Herbert Simon, cited in Christopher Hill, op. cit., p. 1.

46 John Steinbruner, *The Cybernetic Theory of Decision*, Princeton, NJ: Princeton University Press, 1974.

47 Alex Mintz (ed.) *Integrating Cognitive and Rational Theories of Foreign Policy: The Poliheuristic Theory of Decision*, Cambridge: Cambridge University Press, 2004, p. 3.

48 Jonathan Keller and Yi Edward Yang, 'Leadership style, decision context and the poliheuristic theory of decision-making: An experimental analysis', *Journal of Conflict Resolution*, 2008, vol. 52, no. 5, pp. 687–8.

3 Bureaucracies and foreign policy

1 See e.g. Christopher Hill, *The Changing Politics of Foreign Policy*, Basingstoke: Palgrave, 2003, pp. 85–96; Graham T. Allison, 'The Cuban missile crisis' in Steve Smith, Amelia Hadfield and Tim Dunne (eds) *Foreign Policy: Theories, Actors, Cases*, Oxford: Oxford University Press, 2008.

2 Richard E. Neustadt, *Presidential Power: The Politics of Leadership*, New York: Wiley, 1960; Samuel P. Huntington, *The Common Defense: Strategic Programs in National Defense*, New York: Columbia University Press, 1961; Roller W. Schilling, Paul Y. Hammond and, Glenn Herald Snyder, *Strategy, Politics, and Defense Budgets*, New York: Columbia University, Institute of War and Peace Studies, 1962; Michael Crozier, *The Bureaucratic Phenomenon*, Chicago, IL: University of Chicago Press, 1964.

3 Robert J. Art, 'Bureaucratic politics and American foreign policy: A critique', *Policy Sciences*, 1973, no. 4, pp. 468–9.

4 Thomas S. Kuhn, *The Structure of Scientific Revolutions*, University of Chicago Press, 1962, p. 34. On Kuhn's notion of a normal science and its relevance to Allison's work see Miriam Steiner, 'The elusive essence of decision: A critical comparison of Allison's and Snyder's decision-making approaches', *International Studies Quarterly*, 1977, vol. 21, no. 2, pp. 389–422.

5 Graham T. Allison, 'Conceptual models and the Cuban missile crisis', *American Political Science Review*, 1969, vol. 63, no. 3, p. 690.

6 Graham T. Allison and Morton H. Halperin, 'Bureaucratic politics: A paradigm and some policy implications', *World Politics*, 1972, vol. 24, pp. 40–79.

7 On the limited explanatory power of the organizational model for explaining foreign policy change and innovation see Lawrence Freedman, 'Logic, politics and foreign policy processes: A critique of the bureaucratic politics model', *International Affairs*, 1976, vol. 52, no. 3, p. 435; Dan Caldwell, 'Bureaucratic foreign policy-making', *American Behavioral Scientist*, 1977, vol. 21, no. 1, p. 92.

8 David A. Welch, 'The organizational process and bureaucratic politics paradigms: retrospect and prospect', *International Security*, 1992, vol. 17, no. 2, p. 119–146.

9 Allison, op. cit., pp. 698–700.

10 Allison and Halperin, op. cit., p. 56; Art, op. cit., pp. 472–4.

11 Allison, op. cit. pp. 708–12; Morton H. Halperin, 'Why bureaucrats play games?' *Foreign Policy*, 1971, no. 2, pp. 70–90.

12 Freedman, op. cit., p. 437.

13 Allison and Halperin, op. cit., p. 43.

14 Allison and Halperin, op. cit., p. 56.

15 Art, op. cit., p. 474.

16 Steiner, op. cit., p. 402.

17 For a detailed list of these studies see Caldwell, op. cit., p. 102.

18 For a good overview of these critiques see Steve Smith, 'Allison and the Cuban missile crisis: A review of the bureaucratic mode of foreign policy decision-making', *Millennium*, 1980, vol. 9, no. 1, pp. 21–40.

19 Stephen D. Krasner, 'Are bureaucracies important (or Allison Wonder-land)', *Foreign Policy*, 1972, no. 7, pp. 159–79; Art echoes Krasner's claim that the power of the president is understated; Art, op. cit., p. 475.
20 Art, op. cit., pp. 473–90.
21 Freedman, op. cit., pp. 437–41; Caldwell, op. cit., p. 97.
22 Caldwell, op. cit., p. 95.
23 For a critique of the BPM through the notion of 'role' see Martin Hollis and Steve Smith, 'Roles and reasons in foreign policy decision making', *British Journal of Political Science*, 1986, vol. 16, pp. 269–86.
24 Stephen Benedict Dyson, 'Personality and foreign policy: Tony Blair's Iraq decisions', *Foreign Policy Analysis*, 2006, 1986, vol. 2, no. 3, pp. 289–306.
25 Jonathan Bendor and Thomas H. Hammond, 'Rethinking Allison's models', *American Political Science Review*, 1992, vol. 86, no. 2, pp. 314–16.
26 Bendor and Hammond, op. cit., p. 315.
27 Bendor and Hammond, op. cit., p. 317.
28 Jerel A. Rosati, 'Developing a systemic decision-making framework: Bureaucratic politics in perspective', *World Politics*, 1981, vol. 33, no. 2, pp. 234–52.
29 Rosati, op. cit., pp. 248–9.
30 Rosati, op. cit., p. 247.
31 Bendor and Hammond, op. cit., pp. 304–6.
32 David Welch, 'The organizational process and bureaucratic politics para-digms: Retrospect and prospect', *International Security*, 1992, vol. 17, no. 2, especially pp. 119–46.
33 Paul 't Hart and Uriel Rosenthal, 'Reappraising bureaucratic politics', *Mershon International Studies Review*, 1998, vol. 42, no. 2, pp. 236–7.
34 't Hart and Roenthal, op. cit., pp. 234–5.
35 Jutta Weldes, 'Bureaucratic politics: A critical constructivist assessment', *Mershon International Studies Review*, 1998, vol. 42, no. 2, p. 217; Jutta Weldes, *Constructing National Interests: The United States and the Cuban Missile Crisis,* Minneapolis: University of Minnesota Press, 1999.
36 Weldes, 'Bureaucratic politics', p. 218.
37 Weldes, 'Bureaucratic politics', p. 221.
38 Israel is a case in point. For research on the impact of the military on Israeli foreign policy in this context see Oren Barak and Gabriel Sheffer, 'Israel's security network: An exploration of a new approach', *International Journal of Middle East Studies*, 2006, vol. 38, no. 2, pp. 235–61; Yoram Peri, *Generals in the Cabinet Room: How the Military Shapes Israeli Policy*, Washington, DC: The United States Institute for Peace, 2006.
39 Robert O. Keohane, 'International insitutions: two approaches', *International Studies Quarterly*, 1988, vol. 34, no. 4, pp. 379–96.
40 Weldes, 'Bureaucratic politics', p. 222.

4   The domestic sources of foreign policy

1 There is a vast literature on domestic influences and foreign policy. E.g. see James Rosenau (ed.) *Domestic Sources of Foreign Policy*, New York: Free Press, 1967; Peter Katzenstein, 'International relations and domestic structures: Foreign economic policies of advanced industrial states', *International Organization*, 1976, vol. 30, no. 1, pp. 1–45; Peter Gourevitch, 'The

second image reversed: The international sources of domestic politics', *International Organization*, 1978, vol. 32, pp. 881–912; Thomas Risse-Kappen, 'Public opinion, domestic structure and foreign policy in liberal democracies', *World Politics*, 1991, vol. 43, pp. 491–517; Joe Hagan, *Political Opposition and Foreign Policy in Comparative Perspective*, Boulder, CO: Lynne Rienner, 1993; Laura Neack, 'Linking state type with foreign policy behaviour', in Laura Neack, Jeanne Hey, Patrick Haney (eds) *Foreign Policy Analysis: Continuity and Change in its Second Generation*, Englewood Cliffs, NJ: Prentice Hall, 1995; Randolf Rummel, 'Democracies are less warlike than other regimes', *European Journal of International Relations*, 1995, vol. 1, no. 4, pp. 457–79; Maurice East, 'National attributes and foreign policy', in Maurice East, Stephen Salmore and Charles Hermann (eds) *Why Nations Act: Theoretical Perspectives for Comparative Foreign Policy*, Beverly Hills, CA: Sage, 1978; Barbara Salmore and Stephen Salmore, 'Political regimes and foreign policy', in Maurice East, Stephen Salmore and Charles Hermann (eds) *Why Nations Act: Theoretical Perspectives for Comparative Foreign Policy*, Beverly Hills, CA: Sage, 1978.

2 See Mary Kaldor, 'The idea of civil society', *International Affairs*, 2003, vol. 79, no. 3, pp. 583–93.

3 Peter Gourevitch op. cit.

4 Richard Mansbach, Yale Ferguson and Donald Lampert, *The Web of World Politics: Nonstate Actors in the Global System*, Englewood Cliffs; NJ: Prentice Hall, 1976.

5 For two interesting works on the connection between sovereignty and the issues discussed above see Chris Brown, *Sovereignty, Rights and Justice*, Cambridge: Polity, 2002; Stephen Krasner, *Sovereignty: Organized Hypocrisy*, Princeton, NJ: Princeton University Press, 1999.

6 Barry Buzan and Ole Weaver, *Regions and Powers: The Structure of International Security*, Cambridge: Cambridge University Press, 2003.

7 Amitav Acharya, 'How ideas spread? Whose ideas matter – norm localization and institutional change in Asian regionalism', *International Organization*, 2004, vol. 58, no. 2, pp. 239–75.

8 See the works of Michael Barnett and Martha Finnemore.

9 See Peter Katzenstein, op. cit.; Peter Gourevitch, op. cit.; Benjamin Cohen, 'The political economy of international trade', *International Organization*, 1990, vol. 44, no. 2, pp. 261–81; Thomas Risse-Kappen, op. cit.

10 Thomas Risse-Kappen, op. cit.

11 Thomas Risse-Kappen, op. cit.

12 On Kennan's notion of containment and its significance for US foreign policy see, *inter alia*, John L. Gaddis, *Strategies of Containment: A Critical Appraisal of American National Security Policy during the Cold War*, Oxford: Oxford University Press, 2005; Henry Kissinger, *Diplomacy*, New York: Simon and Schuster, 1994, esp. pp. 446–550; Charles Gati and Richard H. Ullman, 'Interview with George F. Kennan', *Foreign Policy*, 1972, no. 7, pp. 5–21; Charles Gati, 'What containment meant, *Foreign Policy*, 1972, no. 7, pp. 22–40.

13 This is most strongly manifested in the lack of influence upon security services, classified material and other unaccountable government branches. See

Fred Halliday, *Rethinking International Relations*, Basingstoke: Macmillan, 1994, p. 84.

14 Michael Doyle, 'Liberalism and world politics', *American Political Science Review*, 1986, vol. 80, pp. 1151–69.

15 Miroslav Ninic, *Democracy and Foreign Policy: The Fallacy of Political Realism*, New York: Columbia University Press, 1992; Christopher Hill, *The Changing Politics of Foreign Policy*, Basingstoke: Palgrave, 2003, pp. 235–40; Thomas Risse-Kappen, op. cit.; Randolph J. Rummel, 'Democracies are less warlike than other regimes', *European Journal of International Relations*, 1995, vol. 1, no. 4, pp. 649–64; Bruce M. Russet, *Grasping the Democratic Peace: Principles for a Post-Cold War World*, Princeton, NJ: Princeton University Press, 1993.

16 Andrew Cooper, Richard Higgott and Kim Nossal, *Relocating Middle Powers: Australia and Canada in a Changing World Order*, Vancouver, BC: University of British Columbia Press, 1993.

17 Donna Lee and James Hamill, 'A middle power paradox? South African diplomacy in the post-apartheid era', *International Relations*, 2001, vol. 15, no. 4, pp. 33–59; Jonathan Ping, Middle Power Statecraft: Indonesia, Malaysia and the Asia-Pacific, Gower, UK: Ashgate Publishers 2005.

18 Stephen Wright (ed.) *African Foreign Policies*, Boulder, CO: Westview Press, 1999; Gilbert M. Khadiagala and Terrence Lyons (eds) *African Foreign Policies: Power and Process*, Boulder, CO: Lynne Rienner, 2001.

19 Two good surveys are Raymond Hinnebusch and Anoushiravan Ehteshami (eds) *The Foreign Policy of Middle East States*, London: Lynne Rienner, 2002; Carl L. Brown (ed.) *Diplomacy in the Middle East: The International Relations of Regional and Outside Powers*, London: I.B. Tauris, 2004.

20 See work by Jurgen Haacke on ASEAN, including Jurgen Haacke and Noel Morada (eds) *Cooperative Security in the Asia-Pacific: The ASEAN Regional Forum*, Oxford: Routledge, 2010; Michael Leifer, *Dictionary of the Modern Politics of Southeast Asia*, Oxford: Routledge, 1995.

21 The key works are Maurice East, op. cit.; Maurice East and Charles Hermann, 'Do nation-types account for foreign policy behaviour?' in James Rosenau (ed.) *Comparing Foreign Policy: Theories, Findings and Methods*, New York: John Wiley, 1974; Barbara Salmore and Stephen Salmore, op. cit.

22 E.g. Randolf Rummel, *National Attributes and Behavior*, Beverley Hills, CA: Sage, 1979.

23 Stephen Krasner, 'Approaches to the state: Alternative conceptions and historical dynamics', *Comparative Politics*, 1984, vol. 16, pp. 223–46.

24 Laura Neack, op. cit.

25 Karl Marx, *The Communist Manifesto,* London: Penguin, 1967, especially chapter 1.

26 Bruce Moon, 'The state in foreign and domestic policy', in Laura Neack, Jeanne Hey and Patrick Haney (eds) *Foreign Policy Analysis: Continuity and Change in its Second Generation*, Englewood Cliffs, NJ: Prentice Hall, 1995, pp. 192–9.

27 Bruce Moon, ibid.

28 Robert W. Cox, *Production, Power and World Order*, Cambridge: Cambridge University Press, 1987; Hein Marais, *South Africa: The Limits to Change*, London: Zed, 2001.

29 David Skidmore and Valerie Hudson (eds) *The Limits of State Autonomy: Society Groups and Foreign Policy Formulation*, Boulder, CO: Westview, 1993, pp 10–11.
30 Christopher Clapham, *Africa and the International System: The Politics of State Survival*, Cambridge: Cambridge University Press, 1996, p. 4.
31 Cited in Michael Clarke, 'Politicians and diplomats', *Parliamentary Affairs*, 1978, vol. 31, no. 1, p. 96.
32 Charles Wright Mills, *The Power Elite*, Oxford: Oxford University Press, 1956.
33 David Skidmore and Valerie Hudson, op. cit., pp. 9–10.
34 The FPA literature on interest groups includes general theoretical works and specific empirical studies though much of it focuses on the US case, e.g. B. Hughes, *The Domestic Context of American Foreign Policy*, San Francisco, CA: W. Freeman, 1978; Richard J. Payne and Eddie Ganaway, 'The influence of black Americans on US policy towards Southern Africa', *African Affairs*, 1980, vol. 79, pp. 567–85; Robert Putnam, 'Diplomacy and domestic politics: The logic of the two-level games', *International Organization*, 1988, vol. 42, no. 3, pp. 427–60; Charles Kegley, *The Domestic Sources of American Foreign Policy*, New York: St Martins Press, 1987; Benjamin Cohen, op. cit.; John Mearsheimer and Stephen M. Walt, *The Israel Lobby*, London: Penguin, 2007.
35 David Skidmore, 'The politics of national security policy: Interest groups, coalitions and the SALT II debate', in David Skidmore and Valerie Hudson, op. cit., pp. 205–32.
36 Christopher Hill, 'Public opinion and British foreign policy', *Millennium*, 1981, vol. 10, no. 1, p. 2.
37 Gabriel Almond, *The American People and Foreign Policy*, New York: Praeger, 1950.
38 Robert Y. Shapiro and Benjamin I. Page, 'Foreign policy and the rational public', *Journal of Conflict Resolution*, 1988, vol. 32, no. 2, pp. 211–47; Thomas W. Graham, 'The pattern and importance of public knowledge in the nuclear age', *Journal of Conflict Resolution*, 1988, vol. 32, no. 2, pp. 319–34.
39 James Rosenau, *Public Opinion and Foreign Policy*, New York: Random House, 1961; see also Ole Holsti, 'Public opinion and foreign policy', *International Studies Quarterly*, 1992, vol. 36, pp. 439–66.
40 Douglas Foyle, 'Public opinion and foreign policy: Elite beliefs as a mediating variable', *International Studies Quarterly*, 1997, vol. 41, no. 1, pp. 141–70.
41 Piers Robinson, 'Theorizing the influence of media on world politics', *European Journal of Communication*, 2001, vol. 16, no. 4, pp. 523–44.
42 Edward Herman and Noam Chomsky, *Manufacturing Consent: The Political Economy of the Mass Media*, New York: Pantheon, 1988.
43 Diane Stone, 'Think tanks – beyond nation states', in Diane Stone and Andrew Denham (eds) *Think Tank Traditions: Policy Research and the Politics of Ideas*, Manchester: Manchester University Press, 2004.
44 Joe Hagan, op. cit.
45 Juliet Kaarbo, 'Power politics in foreign policy: The influence of bureaucratic minorities', *European Journal of International Relations*, 1998, vol. 4, no.1, pp. 67–97.

46 Martin Rochester, 'The paradigm debate in international relations and its implications for foreign policy making: Toward a redefinition of the "national interest"', *Western Political Quarterly*, 1978, vol. 31, no. 1, p. 56.

47 Robert Putnam, op. cit.

48 Robert Keohane and Joseph Nye, *Power and Interdependence: World Politics in Transition*, Boston: Little Brown, 1977.

49 See Michael Pinto-Duchinsky, 'Foreign political aid: The German party foundations and their US counterparts', *International Affairs*, 1991, vol. 67, no. 1, pp. 33–63.

5 Foreign policy analysis and the state

1 Fred Halliday, *Rethinking International Relations*, Basingstoke: Macmillan, 1994, p. 78.

2 Debate on HS and IR began with the work of Fred Halliday, 'State and society in international relations: A second agenda', *Millennium*, 1987, vol. 16, no. 2, pp. 215–30, Anthony Jarvis, 'Societies, states and geopolitics: Challenges from historical sociology', *Review of International Studies*, 1989, vol. 15, no. 3, pp. 281–93 and Michael Banks and Martin Shaw (eds) *State and Society in International Relations*, London: Harvester, 1991. A lively discussion in the *Review of International Political Economy* launched the second debate on HS and IR. See the following exchange: John M. Hobson, 'Debate: The "second wave" of Weberian historical sociology – The historical sociology of the state and the state of historical sociology in international relations', *Review of International Political Economy*, 1998, vol. 5, no. 2, pp. 284–320, Martin Shaw, 'The historical sociology of the future', *Review of International Political Economy*, 1998, vol. 5, no. 2, pp. 321–6, Sandra Halperin, 'Shadowboxing: Weberian historical sociology vs. state-centric international relations theory', *Review of International Political Economy*, 1998, vol. 5, no. 2, pp. 327–39, Hendrik Spruyt, 'Historical sociology and systems theory in international relations', *Review of International Political Economy*, 1998, vol. 5, no. 2, pp. 340–53, John M. Hobson, 'For a "second wave" of Weberian historical sociology in international relations: A reply to Halperin', *Review of International Political Economy*, 1998, vol. 5, no. 2, pp. 354–61. For more recent explorations of the cross-fertilization between HS and IR, see John M. Hobson and Stephen Hobden (eds) *Historical Sociology and International Relations*, Cambridge: Cambridge University Press, 2002; George Lawson, 'The promise of historical sociology in international relations', *International Studies Review*, 2006, vol. 8, no. 3, pp. 397–423.

3 For a notable exception see Fred Halliday, *The Middle East in International Relations*, Cambridge: Cambridge University Press, 2005, pp. 41–75.

4 A classical account is Robert O. Keohane and Joseph S. Nye, *Power and Interdependence*, New York: Longman, 2001.

5 For a dependency theory approach to FPA see Mark Webber and Michael Smith (eds) *Foreign Policy in a Transformed World*, Essex: Prentice Hall, 2002, p. 23. For an interesting debate about applying neo-realism to FPA see Colin Elman, 'Horses for courses: Why *not* neorealist theories of foreign policy?', *Security Studies*, 1996, vol. 6, no. 1, pp. 7–53, Kenneth

Waltz, 'International politics is not foreign policy', *Security Studies,* 1996, vol. 6, no. 1, pp. 54–57, and Colin Elman, 'Cause, effect, and consistency: A response to Kenneth Waltz', *Security Studies,* 1996, vol. 6, no. 1, pp. 58–63.

6 Halliday, *Rethinking International Relations,* pp. 76–8.

7 Anthony Giddens, *The Nation-State and Violence,* London: Polity, 1985; Theda Skocpol, *States and Social Revolutions: A Comparative Analysis of France, Russia, and China,* Cambridge: Cambridge University Press, 1979.

8 Skocpol, op. cit., p. 29.

9 See Halliday, *The Middle East in International Relations,* p. 46.

10 For a succinct exploration of the contribution of Mann's work to IR, see George Lawson et. al., 'The work of Michael Mann', *Millennium,* 2005, vol. 34, no. 2, pp. 476–552 (multiple contributors).

11 Michael Mann, *The Sources of Social Power: The Rise of Classes and Nation-States, 1760–1914,* Cambridge: Cambridge University Press, 1993, p. 55.

12 John M. Hobson, *The State and International Relations,* Cambridge: Cambridge University Press, 2000.

13 Mann, op. cit., p. 59.

14 Ibid.

15 E.g. David Skidmore and Valerie Hudson (eds) *The Limits of State Autonomy: Societal Groups and Foreign Policy* Formulation, Boulder, CO: Westview Press, 1993.

16 Hobson, *The State and International Relations,* p. 201.

17 George Lawson, 'A conversation with Michael Mann', *Millennium,* 2005, vol. 34, no. 2, p. 480.

18 Ibid; Hobson, *The State and International Relations,* p. 201.

19 Hobson, 'Eurocentrism' and neoliberalism in the "Fall of Mann": Will the real Mann please stand up?' *Millennium,* 2005, vol. 34, no. 2, pp. 518–19.

20 Robert H. Jackson, *Quasi-States: Sovereignty, International Relations and the Third World,* Cambridge: Cambridge University Press, 1990, pp. 21–2.

21 Christopher Clapharn, 'Sovereignty and the third world state', *Political Studies,* 1999, vol. 47, p. 522.

22 Jackson, op. cit., pp. 21–2.

23 An international society exists 'when a group of states, conscious of certain common interests and common values, form a society in the sense that they conceive themselves to be bound by a common set of rules in their relations with one another, and share in the working of common institutions', see Headly Bull, *The Anarchical International Society: A Study of Order in World Politics,* London: Macmillan, 1977, p. 13.

24 Robert Jackson, 'Sovereignty in world politics: A glance at the conceptual and historical landscape', *Political Studies,* 1999, vol. 47, p. 431.

25 Jackson, *Quasi-States,* pp. 23–6.

26 Several scholars have examined the evolution of the sovereignty regime from a historical perspective. See Jackson, *Quasi-States,* pp. 32–50; Robert Jackson, 'Sovereignty in world politics'; George Sorenson, 'Sovereignty: Change and continuity in a fundamental institution', *Political Studies,* 1999, vol. 47, pp. 590–604. Our account of the rise of self-determination in

the new sovereignty regime is derived from Clapham's 'Sovereignty and the third world state'.

27 Clapham, 'Sovereignty and the third world state', p. 522.
28 Clapham, 'Sovereignty and the third world state', pp. 522–6.
29 Jean Francois Bayart, 'Africa in the world: A history of extraversion', *African Affairs*, 2000, vol. 99, pp. 217–67.
30 Patrick Chabal and Jean-Pascal Daloz, *Africa Works: The Political Instrumentality of Disorder*, London: Zed, 1999.
31 Jackson, *Quasi-States*, pp. 40–5.
32 See fn 5 for references.
33 We draw on Thomas Risse-Kappen, *Bringing Transnational Relations Back In*, Cambridge: Cambridge University, Press, 1995, p. 6.
34 See, for instance, Gordon A. Craig and Alexander L. George (eds) *Force and Statecraft: Diplomatic Problems of Our Time*, Oxford: Oxford University Press, 1995; Daniel W. Drezner, *The Sanctions Paradox: Economic Statecraft and International Relations*, Cambridge: Cambridge University Press, 1999; Geof W. Berridge, *Diplomacy: Theory and Practice*, Basingstoke: Palgrave, Macmillan, 2005; Joseph S. Nye, *Soft Power: The Means to Success in World Politics*, New York: Public Affairs, 2006.
35 This account draws on a growing literature emphasizing the politico-military origins of changes in contemporary statehood. See, *inter alia*, Tarek Barkawi, *Globalization and War*, Lanham, MD: Rowman & Littlefield, 2006, pp. 1–59; Ian Clark, *Globalization and Fragmentation: International Relations in the Twentieth Century*, Oxford: Oxford University Press, 1997; Ian Clark, *Globalization and International Relations Theory*, Oxford: Oxford University Press, 1999; Martin Shaw, 'The state of globalization: Towards a theory of state transformation', *Review of International Political Economy*, 1997, vol. 4 no. 3, pp. 497–513; Martin Shaw, *Theory of the Global State: Globalization as an Unfinished Revolution*, Cambridge: Cambridge University Press, 2001; Michael Mann, 'Has globalization ended the rise and rise of the nation-state?', *Review of International Political Economy*, 1997, vol. 4 no. 3, pp. 472–96; Michael Mann, 'Globalization and September 11', *New Left Review*, 2001, vol. 12 (Nov.–Dec.), pp. 51–72.
36 For an account of the CW as a conflict between two social systems see Fred Halliday, *The Making of the Second Cold War*, London: Verso, 1986. For the distinction between intra and inter-system dynamics see Clark, *Globalization and Fragmentation*, pp. 121–40.
37 Our line of argument draws on earlier works locating the origins of contemporary globalization in the intra-systemic dynamics of the CW. See Michael Mann, 'As the twentieth century ages', *New Left Review*, 1995, vol. 21 no. 4 (Nov.–Dec.), pp. 104–24; Shaw, *Theory of the Global State;* Shaw, 'The state of globalization'; Clark, *Globalization and International Relations Theory*; Ian Clark, *Globalization and Fragmentation*, pp. 121–40; Daniel Deudney and G. John Ikenberry, 'The nature and sources of liberal international order', *Review of International Studies*, 1999, vol. 25, pp. 179–96.
38 Of course, the political institutionalization of the west faced significant challenges. The US war with Vietnam, Washington's reluctance over West Germany's *ostpolitik*, and the 'uni-lateral withdrawal' of the US from the exchange systems are a few examples. In addition, states and 'their' own societies experienced tensions, e.g. the student mobilization in France in

1968, which further challenges the idea of a politically unified space. The most recent and consequential issue is the Iraq war, which inspired a divisive foreign policy split between the Anglo-American alliance and much of western Europe, echoing the post-CW gap said by Robert Kagan to be emerging. However, despite periodic tensions, the overall political institutionalization of the 'west' has prevailed. For Kagan's account see Robert Kagan, *Paradise and Power: America and Europe in the New World Order*, London: Atlantic, 2003.

39 For the notion of states as 'bordered power containers' see Shaw, 'The state of globalization', pp. 499–500, 506–9.

40 Tarak Barkawi and Mark Laffey, 'The imperial peace: Democracy, force and globalization', *European Journal of International Relations*, 1999, vol. 5, no. 4, pp. 403–34.

41 Shaw, *Theory of the Global State*, p. 244; Morten Ougaard and Richard Higgott, *Towards Global Polity: Future Trends and Prospects*, London: Routledge, 2002.

42 Christopher Hill, *The Changing Politics of Foreign Policy*, Basingstoke: Palgrave, 2003, p. 209.

43 Hill, op. cit., pp. 210–14.

44 There is a wide literature that suggests that the Middle East might be conceived in terms of an institutional state. See, e.g., Halliday, *The Middle East in International Relations*, pp. 42–71; Roger Owen, *State, Power and Politics in the Making of the Modern Middle East*, London: Routledge, 2004; Nazih N. Ayubi, *Overstating the Arab State: Politics and Society in the Middle East*, London: I.B Tauris, 1995, esp. parts 3 and 4.

45 See e.g. Scott Thomas, *The Diplomacy of Liberation: The Foreign Relations of the ANC since 1960*, London: Tauris Academic, 1995.

46 See e.g. Joe Hanlon, *Mozambique: Who Calls the Shots?* London: James Currey, 1991.

47 Alex de Waal, *Famine Crimes: Politics and the Disaster Relief Industry in Africa*, Bloomington: Indiana University Press, 1997.

48 On this point see Halliday, *Rethinking International Relations*, p. 82.

49 For how foreign policy is affected by politico-military structures see the following exchange: Colin Elman, op. cit.; Kenneth Waltz, 'International politics is not foreign policy', *Security Studies*, 1996, vol. 6, no. 1, pp. 54–7; Colin Elman, 'Cause, effect, and consistency: A response to Kenneth Waltz', *Security Studies*, 1996, vol. 6, no. 1, pp. 58–63. The impact of sooio-economic structures has been discussed mainly within dependency theory. For a discussion of dependency theory in the context of FPA, see Mark Webber and Michael Smith, op. cit., p. 23.

6 Foreign policy, globalization and the study of foreign policy analysis

1 David Held, Anthony G. McGrew, David Goldblat and Jonathan Perraton, *Global Transformations: Politics, Economics, Culture*, Cambridge: Polity Press, 1999.

2 For this definition see Christopher Hill, *The Changing Politics of Foreign Policy*, Basingstoke: Palgrave, 2003, p. 3.

3 An examination of the index entries in several works reveals that foreign policy does not appear, e.g. Held et al., op. cit., David Held and Anthony

McGrew (eds) *The Global Transformations Reader*, Cambridge: Polity Press, 2003; Jan Aart Scholte, *Globalization: A Critical Introduction*, London: Palgrave, 2003; Jan Aart Scholte and Ronald Robertson, *Encyclopedia of Globalization*, New York: Routledge, 2007. See also recent forums on GT in *International Politics*, 2005, vol. 42, no. 3, pp. 364–99, and *International Political Sociology*, 2009, vol. 31, no. 1, pp. 109–28.

4 For a classification of GT in these approaches see Held et al., op. cit., pp. 1–29. We focus on the state because foreign policy is usually deemed a key state activity. Thus, the impacts of globalization on the state might be seen as similarly influencing foreign policy.

5 Two good examples representing and enhancing this perception are Thomas L. Friedman, *The World is Flat: A Brief History of the Globalized World in the 21st Century*, London: Allen Lane, 2005; Francis Fukuyama, *The End of History and the Last Man*, London: Penguin, 1993.

6 Held et al., op. cit., p. 2.

7 John Gray, *False Dawn: The Delusions of Global Capitalism*, London: Granta Books, 1998, p. 70.

8 Held et al., op. cit., p. 3.

9 The key global-sceptic text is Paul Hirst and Graham Thompson, *Globalization in Question*, Cambridge: Polity, 2009.

10 Hirst and Thompson, op. cit., pp. 6–7.

11 For this notion of internationalization see Anthony McGrew, 'Globalization and global politics' in John Baylis and Steve Smith (eds) *The Globalization of World Politics*, Oxford: Oxford University Press, 2005, p. 24.

12 Held et al. substantiate this claim empirically in their ground-breaking *Global Transformations*. Also on this point see Jan Aart Scholte, 'Premature obituaries: A response to Justin Rosenberg', *International Politics*, 2005, vol. 42, no. 3, pp. 390–9. For an overview of the challenges and opportunities non-state actors create in world politics see William Wallace and Daphne Josselin (eds) *Non-State Actors in World Politics*, London: Palgrave, 2002.

13 On the significance of Held et al.'s op. cit., work in the context of GT see Joseph S. Nye and Robert O. Keohane, 'Globalization: What's new? What's not? (And so what?)', *Foreign Policy*, 2000, vol. 118, no. 1, pp. 104–20; for the main proponents of the transformationalist thesis see Anthony Giddens, *The Consequences of Modernity*, Cambridge: Polity Press, 1991; Anthony Giddens, *Runaway World*, London: Profile Books, 1999; James N. Rosenau, *Along the Domestic–Foreign Frontier*, Cambridge: Cambridge University Press, 1997; Jan A. Scholte, *Globalization: A Critical Introduction*.

14 Held et al., op. cit., p. 16.

15 Scholte, *Globalization: A Critical Introduction*, p. 46.

16 Ibid.

17 Justin Rosenberg, 'Globalisation theory: a post mortem', *International Politics*, 2005, vol. 42, no. 3, p. 2.

18 Held et al., op. cit., p. 437.

19 Held et al., op. cit., p. 440.

20 Ibid. In similar vein, Scholte argues that globalization has 'reconstructed the state'. Scholte, *Globalization: A Critical Introduction*, pp. 192–214.

21 We draw partly on the argument in Hill, op. cit., pp. 190–1.

22 Held et al., op. cit., p. 41.
23 James N. Rosenau, op. cit., p. 52.
24 Held et al., op. cit., p. 43; Rosenau, op. cit., pp. 81–2; Scholte, *Globalization: A Critical Introduction*, p. 46.
25 We draw on the literature presented in the previous chapter. See Chapter 5, note 35.
26 On the ontological primacy GT attributes to spatio-temporal and economic elements at the expense of other factors, specifically military and political, see Tarek Barkawi, 'Connection and constitution: Locating war and culture in globalization studies', *Globalizations*, 2004, vol. 1, no. 2, pp. 155–70; Martin Shaw, 'The state of globalization: Towards a theory of state transformation', *Review of International Political Economy,* vol. 4, no. 3, 1997, p. 509; Michael Mann, 'Has globalization ended the rise and rise of the nation-state?', *Review of International Political Economy*, vol. 4, no. 3, 1997, p. 493.
27 Shaw, 'The state of globalization', p. 498.
28 See also Ian Clark, *Globalization and International Relations Theory*, Oxford: Oxford University Press, 1999, p. 52; Mann, op. cit., p. 474.
29 Examples included in Brian White, 'Analysing foreign policy problems and approaches', in Michael Clarke and Brian White (eds) *Understanding Foreign Policy*, Cheltenham: Edward Elgar, 1989, p. 3; Walter Carlsnaes, *Ideology and Foreign Policy: Problems of Comparative Conceptualization*, Oxford: Basil Blackwell, 1986, p. 70.
30 On Egypt see Raymond Hinnebusch, 'The foreign policy of Egypt', in Raymond Hinnebusch and Anoushiravan Ehteshami (eds) *The Foreign Policies of Middle East States*, London: Lynne Rienner, 2002; on Israel see Amnon Aran, *Israel's Foreign Policy towards the PLO: The Impact of Globalization*, Sussex: Sussex Academic Press, 2009.
31 For a recent account linking empire-consolidation and globalization see Tarek Barkawi, *Globalization and War*, Lanham, MD: Rowman & Littlefield, 2006, pp. 27–90.
32 On globalization in the context of the global war on terror see, Robert Keohane, 'The globalization of informal violence, theories of world politics, and the liberalism of fear', in Robert O. Keohane (ed.) *Power and Governance in a Partially Globalized World,* London: Routledge, 2002, pp. 272–84.
33 There is an immense literature that accounts for the consolidation of nation-state empires and the international order they generated in the manner described above. See, e.g., Michael Mann, *The Sources of Social Power: The Rise of Classes and Nation-States, 1760–1914*, Cambridge: Cambridge University Press, 1993, p. 504; Phillip Bobit, *The Shield of Achilles*, New York: Anchor Books, 2003, pp. 144–205; Martin Shaw, *Theory of the Global State: Globalization as an Unfinished Revolution*, Cambridge: Cambridge University Press, 2001, p. 104.
34 Daniel Deudney and G. John Ikenberry, 'The nature and sources of liberal international order', *Review of International Studies*, 1999, vol. 25, p. 182.
35 Michael, Mann, 'As the twentieth century ages', *New Left Review,* 1995, vol. 214 (Nov.–Dec.), pp. 104–24.
36 On the role of foreign policy in the construction of liberal spaces see Tarak Barkawi and Mark Laffey, 'The imperial peace: Democracy force and globalization', *European Journal of International Relations*, 1999, vol. 5, no. 4 (esp. pp. 419–23).

7 Foreign policy and change

1 Charles Hermann acknowledged that the ending of the CW brought about a focus on incorporating change in the FPA agenda. Charles Hermann, 'Epilogue: Reflections on foreign policy theory building', in Laura Neack, Jeanne Hey and Patrick Haney (eds) *Foreign Policy Analysis: Continuity and Change in its Second Generation*, Englewood Cliffs, NJ: Prentice Hall, 1995, p. 255. This is despite there being at least one earlier study of the impact of major system change on foreign policy alignments, K.J. Holsti, *Why Nations Realign: Foreign Policy Restructuring in a Post-War World*, London: Allen and Unwin, 1982. See also Jerel Rosati, Joe Hagan and Martin Sampson (eds) *Foreign Policy Restructuring*, Columbia: University of South Carolina, 1994.

2 Margaret Hermann, 'Indicators of stress in policymakers during foreign policy crises', *Political Psychology*, 1979, vol. 1, no. 1, p. 1.

3 Charles Hermann, 'Changing course: When governments choose to redirect foreign policy', *International Studies Quarterly*, 1990, vol. 34, no. 1, pp. 5–6.

4 See David Welch, *Painful Choices: A Theory of Foreign Policy Change*, Princeton, NJ: Princeton University Press, 2005.

5 David Welch, op. cit., p. 8.

6 David Welch, op. cit., p. 22.

7 Charles Hermman, Margaret Hermann and Joe Hagan, 'How decision units shape foreign policy behavior', in Charles Hermann, Charles Kegley and James Rosenau (eds) *New Directions in the Study of Foreign Policy*, London: Allen & Unwin, 1987.

8 Daniel Byman and Kenneth M. Pollack, 'Let us now praise great men: Bringing the statesman back in', *International Security,* 2001, vol. 25, no. 4, pp. 107–46.

9 See, e.g., the work on Gorbechev, such as Janice Stein, 'Political learning by doing: Gorbachev as uncommitted thinker and motivated learner', *International Organization*, 1994, vol. 48, no. 2. pp. 155–83; for a contrasting depiction, see Jeffrey Checkel, 'Ideas, institutions and the Gorbachev foreign policy revolution', *World Politics*, 1993, vol. 45, no. 2, pp. 271–300.

10 Jack Levy, 'Learning and foreign policy: Sweeping a conceptual minefield', *International Organization*, 1994, vol. 48, no. 2, pp. 279–312; Janice Stein, op. cit.

11 Wang Jisi, 'China's search for a grand strategy: A rising power finds its way', *Foreign Affairs*, 2011, vol. 90, no. 2, pp. 74–7.

12 See Gregory Chin and Ramesh Thakur, 'Will China change the rules of global order?' *Washington Quarterly*, 2010, vol. 33, no. 4, pp. 119–38; Alastair Johnston, 'Is China a status quo power?' *International Security*, 2003, vol. 7, no. 4, pp. 5–56.

13 For an overview of the topic, see Karen Smith, *European Union Foreign Policy in a Changing World,* Cambridge: Polity, 2008.

14 Yaacov Vertzberger, 'Foreign policy decision-makers as practical intuitive historians: Applied history and its shortcomings', *International Studies Quarterly*, 1986, vol. 30, no. 2, pp. 223–47.

15 Yuen Foong Khong, *Analogies at War: Korea, Munich, Diem Bien Phu and the Vietnam Decisions of 1965*, Princeton, NJ: Princeton University Press, 1992.

16 Yuen Foong Khong, op. cit., pp. 20–1.

17 Elisabetta Brighi and Christopher Hill, 'Implementation and behaviour', in Steve Smith, Amanda Hatfield and Tim Dunne (eds) *Foreign Policy: Theories, Actors, Cases,* Oxford: Oxford University Press, 2008, pp. 117–36.

18 David Skidmore, 'The politics of national security policy: Interest groups, coalitions and the SALT II debates', in David Skidmore and Valerie Hudson (eds) *The Limits of State Autonomy: Societal Groups and Foreign Policy Formulation,* Boulder, CO: Westview, 1993.

19 K.J. Holsti, op. cit.

20 Michael Barnett, 'Culture, strategy and foreign policy change: Israel's road to Oslo', *European Journal of International Relations,* 1999, vol. 5, no. 1, pp. 5–36.

21 Sypros Blavokos and Dimitris Bourantonis, 'Accounting for foreign policy change: The role of policy entrepreneurs', paper presented at SGIR Pan-European Conference on IR, September, 2010.

22 Joe Hagan, 'Domestic political explanations in the analysis of foreign policy', in Laura Neack, Jeanne Hey and Patrick Haney (eds) *Foreign Policy Analysis: Continuity and Change in its Second Generation,* Englewood Cliffs, NJ: Prentice Hall, 1995, p. 138.

23 Brian Ripley, 'Cognition, culture and bureaucratic politics' in Neack et al., op. cit., pp. 91–4.

24 Juliet Kaarbo, 'Power politics in foreign policy: The influence of bureaucratic minorities', *European Journal of International Relations,* 1998, vol. 4, no. 1, pp. 67–99.

25 Andreas Mehler, 'Eternal plight: France in search of a new Africa policy', *Spiegel Online International,* 4 November 2008, www.spiegel.de/international/world/0c1518,546796,00.html, accessed 5 April 2011.

26 Chris Alden, 'From liberation movement to political party: ANC foreign policy in transition', *South African Journal of International Affairs,* 1993, vol. 1, no. 1, pp. 80–95.

27 See, e.g., Stephen Gerras, 'The army as a learning organization', www.ai.dtic.mil/oai, Army War College, Carlisle, PA, 2002; Davis Bobrow, *Adaptive Politics, Social Learning and Military Institutions,* Springfield, VA: National Technical Information Service, 1970; John Shy, 'The American military experience: History and learning', *Journal of Interdisciplinary History,* 1971, vol. 1, no. 2, pp. 205–28.

28 Peter Haas, 'Introduction: Epistemic communities and international policy coordination', *International Organization,* 1992, vol. 46, no. 1, pp. 1–35.

29 Yuen Foong Khong, 'Neoconservatism and the domestic sources of American foreign policy: The role of ideas in Operation Iraqi Freedom' in Smith et al., op. cit., 2008.

30 B. Guy Peters, *Institutional Theory in Political Science: The 'New Institutionalism',* 2nd edn, London: Continuum, 2005.

31 George Downs and David Rocke, 'Conflict, agency and gambling for resurrection: The principal-agent problem goes to war', *American Journal of Political Science,* 1994, vol. 38, no. 2, p. 362.

32 See, e.g., Ian Johnston, 'The role of the UN Secretary General: The power of persuasion based on law', *Global Governance,* 2003, vol. 9, no. 4, pp. 441–59; Terrence Chapman and Dan Reiter, 'The United Nations Security Council and the rally round the flag effect', *Journal of Conflict Resolution,* 2004, vol. 48, pp. 886–909; Imelda Maher, Stijn Billiet and

140   *Notes*

Dermot Hodson, 'The principal-agent approach to EU studies: Apply liberally but handle with care', *Comparative European Politics*, 2009, vol. 7, no. 4, pp. 409–13; Michael Lipson, 'Between Iraq and a hard place: UN arms inspections and the politics of Security Council Resolution 1441', paper presented at Midwest Political Science Association, 20 April, 2006.

33 Samuel Huntington, *The Third Wave: Democratization in the Late Twentieth Century*, Norman: Oklahoma University Press, 1991; Juan Linz 'Transitions to democracy', *Washington Quarterly*, 1990, vol. 13, no. 3, pp. 133–42; Juan Linz and Alfred Stepan, *Problems of Transition and Consolidation*, Baltimore, MD: Johns Hopkins University Press, 1996.

34 Alison Stanger, 'Democratization and the international system', in Miles Kahler (ed.) *Liberalization and Foreign Policy*, New York: Columbia University Press, 1997.

35 Paulo Gorjao, 'Regime change and foreign policy: Portugal, Indonesia and the self-determination of East Timor', *Democratization*, 2002, vol. 9, no. 4, pp. 142–58.

36 Edward Mansfield and Jack Snyder, 'Democratisation and war', *Foreign Affairs*, 1995, May/June, pp. 79–97; Edward Mansfield and Jack Snyder, *Electing to Fight: Why Emerging Democracies Go To War*, Cambridge, MA: MIT Press, 2005.

37 Valerie Philip Gagnon, 'Ethnic nationalism and international conflict: The case of Serbia', *International Security*, 1993/94, vol. 19, no. 3, pp. 130–66.

38 Judith Goldstein and Robert Keohane (eds) *Ideas and Foreign Policy: Beliefs, Institutions and Political Change*, Ithaca, NY: Cornell University Press, 1993.

39 Fred Halliday, *Revolution and World Politics: The Rise and Fall of the Sixth Great Power*, Basingstoke: Palgrave, 1999; David Armstrong, *Revolution and World Order: The Revolutionary State in International Society*, Oxford: Blackwell, 1993.

40 Halliday, op. cit., p. 156.

41 Chris Alden, *Mozambique and the Construction of the New African State*, Basingstoke: Palgrave, 2001, p. 7.

42 Miles Kahler, 'Conclusion: Liberalization as foreign policy determinant and goal', in Miles Kahler (ed.) *Liberalization and Foreign Policy*, New York: Columbia University Press, 1997.

43 Paulo Gorjao, op. cit.

44 See David Campbell, *Writing Security: United States Foreign Policy and the Politics of Identity*, Minneapolis: University of Minnesota, 1992.

45 David Campbell, op. cit., pp. 11–12.

46 Chris Alden and Garth le Pere, *South Africa's Post-Apartheid Foreign Policy – From Reconciliation to Revival?* Adelphi Paper 362, Oxford: Oxford University Press, 2003.

8 Conclusion: new directions in foreign policy analysis

1 Bahgat Korany, 'Analyzing Third World foreign policies; a critique and re-ordered research agenda', in David Wurfel and Bruce Burton (eds) *The Political Economy of Foreign Policy in Southeast Asia*, Basingstoke: Macmillan, 1990, pp. 24–30.

2 Barry Buzan and Richard Little, *International Systems in World History,* Oxford: Oxford University Press, 2000.
3 The works by David Houghton and Jeff Checkel being the principal exceptions.
4 Wang Jisi, 'China's search for a grand strategy: A rising power finds its way', *Foreign Affairs,* 2011, vol. 90, no. 2, p. 76.

Bibliography

Acharya, Amitav, 'How ideas spread? Whose ideas matter – norm localisation and institutional change in Asian regionalism', *International Organization,* 2004, vol. 58, pp. 239–75.

Albert, Mathias, '"Globalisation theory" Yesterday's fad or more lively than ever?', *International Political Sociology,* 2007, vol. 2, pp. 165–82.

Alden, Chris, 'From liberation movement to political party: ANC foreign policy in transition', *South African Journal of International Affairs,* 1993, vol. 1, no. 1, pp. 80–95.

——, *Mozambique and the Construction of the New African State,* Basingstoke: Palgrave, 2001.

Alden, Chris and Garth le Pere, *South Africa's Post-Apartheid Foreign Policy – From Reconciliation to Revival?* Adelphi Paper 362, Oxford: Oxford University Press, 2003.

Allison, Graham T., 'Conceptual models and the Cuban missile crisis', *American Political Science Review,* 1969, vol. 63, no. 3, pp. 689–718.

——, *Essence of decision: explaining the Cuban missile crisis,* 2nd edn, Boston: Little Brown, 1971.

——, 'The Cuban missile crisis', in Steve Smith, Amelia Hadfield and Tim Dunne (eds) *Foreign Policy: Theories, Actors, Cases,* Oxford: Oxford University Press, 2008.

Allison, Graham T. and Morton H. Halperin, 'Bureaucratic politics: A paradigm and some policy implications', *World Politics,* 1972, vol. 24, pp. 40–79.

Almond, Gabriel, *The American People and Foreign Policy,* New York: Praeger, 1950.

Aran, Amnon, *Israel's Foreign Policy towards the PLO: The Impact of Globalization,* Sussex: Sussex Academic Press, 2009.

Archibald, Kathleen (ed.), *Strategic Interaction and Conflict,* Berkeley: University of California Press, 1966.

Armstrong, David, *Revolution and World Order: The Revolutionary State in International Society,* Oxford: Blackwell, 1993.

Art, Robert J., 'Bureaucratic politics and American foreign policy: A critique', *Policy Sciences,* 1973, no. 4, pp. 467–90.

Axelrod, Robert (ed.), *Structure of Decision: The Cognitive Maps of Political Elites*, Princeton, NJ: Princeton University Press, 1976.

Ayubi, Nazih N., *Overstating the Arab State: Politics and Society in the Middle East*, London: I.B. Tauris, 1995.

Banks, Michael and Martin Shaw (eds), *State and Society in International Relations*, London: Harvester, 1991.

Barak, Oren and Gabriel Sheffer, 'Israel's security network: An exploration of a new approach', *International Journal of Middle East Studies*, 2006, vol. 38, no. 2, pp. 235–61.

Barkawi, Tarek, 'Connection and constitution: Locating war and culture in globalization studies', *Globalizations*, 2004, vol. 1, no. 2, pp. 155–70.

——, *Globalization and War*, Lanham, MD: Rowman & Littlefield, 2006.

Barkawi, Tarek and Mark Laffey, 'The imperial peace: Democracy, force and globalization', *European Journal of International Relations*, 1999, vol. 5, no. 4, pp. 403–34.

Barnett, Michael, 'Culture, strategy and foreign policy change: Israel's road to Oslo', *European Journal of International Relations*, 1999, vol. 5, no. 1, pp. 5–36.

Barnett, Michael and Martha Finnemore, Rules for the World: International Organizations in Global Politics, Syracuse, NY: Cornell University Press, 2004.

Bayart, Jean Francois, 'Africa in the world: A history of extraversion', *African Affairs*, 2000, vol. 99, pp. 217–67.

Bendor, Jonathan and Thomas H. Hammond, 'Rethinking Allison's models', *American Political Science Review*, 1992, vol. 86, no. 2, pp. 301–22.

Bernstein, Barton, 'The Cuban missile crisis: Trading the Jupiters in Turkey?' *Political Science Quarterly*, 1980, vol. 95, no. 1, pp. 97–125.

Berridge, Geof W. *Diplomacy: Theory and Practice*, Basingstoke: Palgrave, Macmillan, 2005.

Blavokos, Sypros and Dimitris Bourantonis, 'Accounting for foreign policy change: The role of policy entrepreneurs', paper presented at the Standing Group on International Relations, Pan-European Conference on IR, September, 2010.

Bobit, Phillip, *The Shield of Achilles*, New York: Anchor Books, 2003.

Bobrow, Davis, *Adaptive Politics, Social Learning and Military Institutions*, Springfield, VA: National Technical Information Service, 1970.

Boulding, Kenneth, *The Image: Knowledge in Life and Society*, Ann Arbor, MI: Arbor Paperbacks, 1956.

——, 'National images and international systems' *Journal of Conflict Resolution*, 1959, vol. 3, pp. 120–31.

Brighi, Elisabetta and Christopher Hill, 'Implementation and behaviour', in Steve Smith, Amanda Hatfield and Tim Dunne (eds) *Foreign Policy: Theories, Actors, Cases*, Oxford: Oxford University Press, 2008, pp. 117–36.

Brown, Carl L. (ed.), *Diplomacy in the Middle East: The International Relations of Regional and Outside Powers*, London: I.B. Tauris, 2004.

Brown, Chris, *Sovereignty, Rights and Justice*, Cambridge: Polity, 2002.

Bull, Headly, *The Anarchical International Society: A Study of Order in World Politics*, London: Macmillan, 1977.

Buzan, Barry and Richard Little, *International Systems in World History*, Oxford: Oxford University Press, 2000.

Buzan, Barry and Ole Weaver, *Regions and Powers: The Structure of International Security*, Cambridge: Cambridge University Press, 2003.

Byman, Daniel and Kenneth M. Pollack, 'Let us now praise great men: Bringing the statesman back in', *International Security*, 2001, vol. 25, no. 4, pp. 107–46.

Caldwell, Dan, 'Bureaucratic foreign policy-making', *American Behavioral Scientist*, 1977, vol. 21, no. 1, pp. 87–110.

Campbell, David, *Writing Security: United States Foreign Policy and the Politics of Identity*, Minneapolis: University of Minnesota, 1992.

Caporaso, James A., 'Across the great divide: Integrating comparative and international politics', *International Studies Quarterly*, 1997, vol. 41, no. 4, pp. 563–91.

Carlsnaes, Walter, *Ideology and Foreign Policy: Problems of Comparative Conceptualization*, Oxford: Basil Blackwell, 1986.

——, 'The agency-structure problem in foreign policy analysis', *International Studies Quarterly*, 1992, vol. 36, no. 3, pp. 245–70.

Chabal, Patrick and Jean-Pascal Daloz, *Africa Works: The Political Instrumentality of Disorder*, London: Zed, 1999.

Chapman, Terrence and Dan Reiter, 'The United Nations Security Council and the rally round the flag effect', *Journal of Conflict Resolution*, 2004, vol. 48, pp. 886–909.

Checkel, Jeffrey, 'Ideas, institutions and the Gorbachev foreign policy revolution', *World Politics*, 1993, vol. 45, no. 2, pp. 271–300.

Chin, Gregory and Thakur, Ramesh, 'Will China change the rules of global order?' *Washington Quarterly*, 2010, vol. 33, no. 4, pp. 119–38.

Clapham, Christopher, *Africa and the International System: The Politics of State Survival*, Cambridge: Cambridge University Press, 1996.

——, 'Sovereignty and the third world state', *Political Studies*, 1999, vol. 47, pp. 522–37.

Clark, Ian, *Globalization and Fragmentation: International Relations in the Twentieth Century*, Oxford: Oxford University Press, 1997.

——, *Globalization and International Relations Theory*, Oxford: Oxford University Press, 1999.

Clarke, Michael, 'Politicians and diplomats', *Parliamentary Affairs*, 1978, vol. 31, no. 1, pp. 96–8.

Cohen, Benjamin, 'The political economy of international trade', *International Organization*, 1990, vol. 44, no. 2, pp. 261–81.

Cooper, Andrew, Richard Higgott and Kim Nossal, *Relocating Middle Powers: Australia and Canada in a Changing World Order*, Vancouver, BC: University of British Columbia Press, 1993.

Cox, Robert W., *Production, Power and World Order*, Cambridge: Cambridge University Press, 1987.

Craig, Gordon A. and Alexander L. George (eds), *Force and State-craft: Diplomatic Problems of Our Time*, Oxford: Oxford University Press, 1995.

Crozier, Michael, *The Bureaucratic Phenomenon*, Chicago, IL: University of Chicago Press, 1964.

Deudney, Daniel and G. John Ikenberry, 'The nature and sources of liberal international order', *Review of International Studies*, 1999, vol. 25, pp. 179–96.

Downs, George and David Rocke, 'Conflict, agency and gambling for resurrection: The principal-agent problem goes to war', *American Journal of Political Science*, 1994, vol. 38, no. 2, pp. 362–80.

Doyle, Michael, 'Liberalism and world politics', *American Political Science Review*, 1986, vol. 80, pp. 1151–69.

Drezner, Daniel W., *The Sanctions Paradox: Economic Statecraft and International Relations*, Cambridge: Cambridge University Press, 1999.

Dyson, Stephen, 'Personality and foreign policy: Tony Blair's Iraq decision', *Foreign Policy Analysis*, 2006, vol. 2, pp. 289–306.

East, Maurice, 'National attributes and foreign policy', in Maurice East, Stephen Salmore and Charles Hermann (eds) *Why Nations Act: Theoretical Perspectives for Comparative Foreign Policy*, Beverly Hills, CA: Sage, 1978.

East, Maurice and Charles Hermann, 'Do nation-types account for foreign policy behaviour?' in James Rosenau (ed.) *Comparing Foreign Policy: Theories, Findings and Methods*, New York: John Wiley, 1974.

Elman, Colin, 'Cause, effect, and consistency: A response to Kenneth Waltz', *Security Studies*, 1996, vol. 6, no. 1, pp. 58–63.

——, 'Horses for courses: Why *not* neorealist theories of foreign policy?', *Security Studies*, 1996, vol. 6, no. 1, pp. 7–53.

Evans, Peter B., Harold K. Jacobson and Robert D. Putnam (eds), *Double-Edged Diplomacy*, Berkeley: University of California Press, 1993.

Fiske, Susan and Shelley Taylor, *Social Cognition*, New York: McGraw-Hill, 1984.

Foyle, Douglas, 'Public opinion and foreign policy: Elite beliefs as a mediating variable', *International Studies Quarterly*, 1997, vol. 41, no. 1, pp. 141–70.

Freedman, Lawrence, 'Logic, politics and foreign policy processes: A critique of the bureaucratic politics model', *International Affairs*, 1976, vol. 52, no. 3, pp. 434–49.

Friedman, Thomas L., *The World is Flat: A Brief History of the Globalized World in the 21st Century*, London: Allen Lane, 2005.

Fukuyama, Francis, *The End of History and the Last Man*, London: Penguin, 1993.

Gaddis, John L., *Strategies of Containment: A Critical Appraisal of American National Security Policy during the Cold War*, Oxford: Oxford University Press, 2005.

Gagnon, Valerie Philip, 'Ethnic nationalism and international conflict: The case of Serbia', *International Security*, 1993/94, vol. 19, no. 3, pp. 130–66.

Gati, Charles, 'What containment meant', *Foreign Policy*, 1972, no. 7, pp. 22–40.

Gati, Charles and Richard H. Ullman, 'Interview with George F. Kennan', *Foreign Policy*, 1972, no. 7, pp. 5–21.

George, Alexander, 'The "Operational Code": A neglected approach to the study of political leaders and decision-making', *International Studies Quarterly*, 1969, vol. 13, no. 2, pp. 190–222.

——, 'The case for multiple advocacy in making foreign policy', *American Political Science Review*, 1972, vol. 66, no. 3, pp. 731–85.

Gerras, Stephen, 'The army as a learning organization', www.ai.dtic.mil/oai, Army War College, Carlisle, PA.

Giddens, Anthony, *The Nation-State and Violence*, London: Polity, 1985.

——, *The Consequences of Modernity*, Cambridge: Polity Press, 1991.

——, *Runaway World*, London: Profile Books, 1999.

Goldstein, Judith and Robert Keohane (eds), *Ideas and Foreign Policy: Beliefs, Institutions and Political Change*, Ithaca, NY: Cornell University Press, 1993.

Gorjao, Paulo, 'Regime change and foreign policy: Portugal, Indonesia and the self-determination of East Timor', *Democratization*, 2002, vol. 9, no. 4, pp. 142–58.

Gourevitch, Peter 'The second image reversed: The international sources of domestic politics', *International Organization*, 1978, vol. 32, pp. 881–912.

Graham, Thomas W., 'The pattern and importance of public knowledge in the nuclear age', *Journal of Conflict Resolution*, 1988, vol. 32, no. 2, pp. 319–34.

Gray, John, *False Dawn: The Delusions of Global Capitalism*, London: Granta Books, 1998.

Gross Stein, Janice, 'Foreign policy decision making: Rational, psychological and neurological models', in Steven Smith, Amelia Hadfield and Timothy Dunne (eds) *Foreign Policy: Theories, Actors, Cases*, Oxford: Oxford University Press, 2008.

Haacke, Jurgen and Noel Morada (eds), *Cooperative Security in the Asia-Pacific: The ASEAN Regional Forum*, Oxford: Routledge, 2010.

Haas, Peter, 'Introduction: epistemic communities and international policy coordination', *International Organization*, 1992, vol. 46, no. 1, pp. 1–35.

Hagan, Joe, *Political Opposition and Foreign Policy in Comparative Perspective*, Boulder, CO: Lynne Rienner, 1993.

——, 'Domestic political explanations in the analysis of foreign policy', in Laura Neack, Jeanne Hey and Patrick Haney (eds) *Foreign Policy Analysis: Continuity and Change in its Second Generation*, Englewood Cliffs, NJ: Prentice Hall, 1995.

Halliday, Fred, *The Making of the Second Cold War*, London: Verso, 1986.

——, 'State and society in international relations: A second agenda', *Millennium*, 1987, vol. 16, no. 2, pp. 215–30.

——, *Rethinking International Relations*, Basingstoke: Macmillan, 1994.

——, *Revolution and World Politics: The Rise and Fall of the Sixth Great Power*, Basingstoke: Palgrave, 1999.

——, *The Middle East in International Relations*, Cambridge: Cambridge University Press, 2005.

Halperin, Morton H., 'Why bureaucrats play games?' *Foreign Policy*, 1971, no. 2, pp. 70–90.

Halperin, Sandra, 'Shadowboxing: Weberian historical sociology vs. state-centric international relations theory', *Review of International Political Economy*, 1998, vol. 5, no. 2, pp. 327–39.

Hanlon, Joe, *Mozambique: Who Calls the Shots?* London: James Currey, 1991.

Held, David and Anthony McGrew (eds), *The Global Transformations Reader*, Cambridge: Polity Press, 2003.

Held, David and Anthony McGrew (eds), *Globalisation Theory: Approaches and Controversies*, Cambridge: Polity Press, 2007.

Held, David, Anthony G. McGrew, David Goldblat and Jonathan Perraton, *Global Transformations: Politics, Economics, Culture*, Cambridge: Polity Press, 1999.

Hermann, Charles, 'Changing course: When governments choose to redirect foreign policy', *International Studies Quarterly*, 1990, vol. 34, no. 1, pp. 3–21.

——, 'Epilogue: Reflections on foreign policy theory building', in Laura Neack, Jeanne Hey and Patrick Haney (eds), *Foreign Policy Analysis: Continuity and Change in its Second Generation*, Englewood Cliffs, NJ: Prentice Hall 1995.

Hermann, Charles, Margaret Hermann and Joe Hagan, 'How decision units shape foreign policy behavior', in Charles Hermann, Charles Kegley and James Rosenau (eds), *New Directions in the Study of Foreign Policy*, London: Allen & Unwin, 1987.

Herman, Edward and Noam Chomsky, *Manufacturing Consent: The Political Economy of the Mass Media*, New York: Pantheon, 1988.

Hermann, Margaret, 'Indicators of stress in policymakers during foreign policy crises', *Political Pschology*, 1979, vol. 1, no. 1, pp. 27–46.

Higgot, Donna Lee and James Hamill, 'A middle power paradox? South African diplomacy in the post-apartheid era', *International Relations*, 2001, vol. 15, no. 4, pp. 33–59.

Hill, Christopher, 'Public opinion and British foreign policy', *Millennium*, 1981, vol. 10, no. 1, pp. 53–62.

——, 'What is left of the domestic?' in Michi Ebata (ed.), *Confronting the Political in International Relations*, London: Macmillan, 2000.

——, *The Changing Politics of Foreign Policy*, Basingstoke: Palgrave, 2003.

Hinnebusch, Raymond and Anoushiravan Ehteshami (eds), *The Foreign Policy of Middle East States*, London: Lynne Rienner, 2002.

Hirst, Paul and Graham Thompson, *Globalization in Question*, Cambridge: Polity, 2009.

Hobson, John M., 'Debate: The "second wave" of Weberian historical sociology – The historical sociology of the state and the state of historical sociology in international relations', *Review of International Political Economy*, 1998, vol. 5, no. 2, pp. 284–320.

——, 'For a "second wave" of Weberian historical sociology in international relations: A reply to Halperin', *Review of International Political Economy*, 1998, vol. 5, no. 2, pp. 354–61.

——, '"Eurocentrism" and neoliberalism in the "Fall of Mann": Will the real Mann please stand up?' *Millennium*, 2005, vol. 34, no. 2, pp. 517–27.

——, *The State and International Relations*, Cambridge: Cambridge University Press, 2000.

Hobson, John M. and Stephen Hobden (eds), *Historical Sociology and International Relations*, Cambridge: Cambridge University Press, 2002.

Hollis, Martin and Steve Smith, 'Roles and reasons in foreign policy decision making', *British Journal of Political Science*, 1986, vol. 16, no. 3, pp. 269–86.

Holsti, K.J., *Why Nations Realign: Foreign Policy Restructuring in a Post-war World*, London: Allen and Unwin, 1982.

Holsti, Ole, 'The belief system and national images: A case study', *Journal of Conflict Resolution*, 1962, vol. 6, no. 3, pp. 244–52.

——, 'The operational code approach to the study of political leaders: John Foster Dulles' philosophical and instrumental beliefs', *Canadian Journal of Political Science*, vol. 3, no. 1, 1970, pp. 123–57.

——, 'Foreign policy formation viewed cognitively', in Robert Axelrod (ed.), *Structure of Decision: The Cognitive Maps of Political Elites*, Princeton, NJ: Princeton University Press, 1976.

——, 'Public opinion and foreign policy', *International Studies Quarterly*, 1992, vol. 36, pp. 439–66.

Houghton, David Patrick, 'Reinvigorating the study of foreign policy decision making: Toward a constructivist approach', *Foreign Policy Analysis*, 2007, vol. 3, no. 1, pp. 24–45.

Hudson, Valerie M. 'Foreign policy analysis: Actor-specific theory and the ground of international relations', *Foreign Policy Analysis*, 2005, vol. 1, no. 1, pp. 1–30.

——, *Foreign Policy Analysis: Classic and Contemporary Theory*, Lanham, MD: Rowman & Littlefield, 2007.

Hughes, B., *The Domestic Context of American Foreign Policy*, San Francisco, CA: W. Freeman, 1978.

Huntington, Samuel P. *The Common Defense: Strategic Programs in National Defense*, New York: Columbia University Press, 1961.

——, 'Transnational organizations in world politics', *World Politics*, 1973, vol. 25, no. 3, pp. 333–68.

——, *The Third Wave: Democratization in the Late Twentieth Century*, Norman: Oklahoma University Press, 1991.

Iieda, Keisuke, 'When and how do domestic constraints matter: Two-level games with uncertainty', *Journal of Conflict Resolution*, 1993, vol. 37, no. 2, pp. 403–26.

Jackson, Robert H., *Quasi-States: Sovereignty, International Relations and the Third World*, Cambridge: Cambridge University Press, 1990.

——, 'Sovereignty in world politics: A glance at the conceptual and historical landscape', *Political Studies*, 1999, vol. 47, pp. 431–56.

Janis, Irving, *Groupthink: Psychological Studies of Policy Decisions and Fiascos*, Boston, MA: Houghton Mifflin, 1982.

Janis, Irving and Leon Mann, *Decision Making*, New York: Free Press, 1977.

Jarvis, Anthony, 'Societies, states and geopolitics: Challenges from historical sociology', *Review of International Studies*, 1989, vol. 15, no. 3, pp. 281–93.

Jensen, Lloyd, *Explaining Foreign Policy*, Englewood Cliffs, NJ: Prentice Hall, 1982.

Jervis, Robert, 'Hypotheses on misperception', *World Politics*, 1968, vol. 20, no. 3, pp. 454–79.

——, *Perception and Misperception in International Politics*, Princeton, NJ: Princeton University Press, 1976.

Jisi, Wang, 'China's search for a grand strategy: A rising power finds its way' *Foreign Affairs*, 2011, vol. 90, no. 2, pp. 74–7.

Johnston, Alastair 'Is China a status quo power?' *International Security*, 2003, vol. 7, no. 4, pp. 5–56.

Johnston, Ian 'The role of the UN Secretary General: The power of persuasion based on law', *Global Governance*, 2003, vol. 9, no. 4, pp. 441–59.

Jones, Roy E., *Principles of Foreign Policy – The Civil State in its World Setting*, Oxford: Martin Robertson, 1979.

Josselin, Daphne and William Wallace (eds), *Non-State Actors in World Politics*, London: Palgrave, 2001.

Kaarbo, Juliet, 'Power politics in foreign policy: The influence of bureaucratic minorities', *European Journal of International Relations*, 1998, vol. 4, no. 1, pp. 67–97.

Kagan, Robert, *Paradise and Power: America and Europe in the New World Order*, London: Atlantic, 2003.

Kahler, Miles, 'Conclusion: Liberalization as foreign policy determinant and goal', in Miles Kahler (ed.), *Liberalization and Foreign Policy*, New York: Columbia University Press, 1997.

Kaldor, Mary, 'The idea of civil society', *International Affairs*, 2003, vol. 79, no. 3, pp. 583–93.

Katzenstein, Peter, 'International relations and domestic structures: Foreign economic policies of advanced industrial states', *International Organization*, 1976, vol. 30, no. 1, pp. 1–45.

Kegley, Charles, *The Domestic Sources of American Foreign Policy*, New York: St Martin's Press, 1987.

Keller, Jonathan and Yi Edward Yang, 'Leadership style, decision context and the poliheuristic theory of decision-making: An experimental analysis', *Journal of Conflict Resolution*, 2008, vol. 52, no. 5, pp. 687–8.

Keohane, Robert O., 'International insitutions: two approaches', *International Studies Quarterly*, 1988, vol. 34, no. 4, pp. 379–96.

——, 'The globalization of informal violence, theories of world politics, and the liberalism of fear', in Robert O. Keohane (ed.), *Power and Governance in a Partially Globalized World,* London: Routledge, 2002, pp. 272–84.

Keohane, Robert O. and Joseph Nye, *Power and Interdependence: World Politics in Transition,* Boston: Little Brown, 1977.

Keohane, Robert O. and Joseph S. Nye, *Power and Interdependence,* New York: Longman, 2001.

Khadiagala, Gilbert M. and Terrence Lyons (eds), *African Foreign Policies: Power and Process,* Boulder, CO: Lynne Rienner, 2001.

Khong, Yuen Foong, *Analogies at War: Korea, Munich, Diem Bien Phu and the Vietnam Decisions of 1965,* Princeton, NJ: Princeton University Press, 1992.

——, 'Neoconservatism and the domestic sources of American foreign policy: The role of ideas in Operation Iraqi Freedom', in Steven Smith, Amelia Hadfield and Timothy Dunne (eds) *Foreign Policy: Theories, Actors, Cases,* Oxford: Oxford University Press, 2008.

Kissinger, Henry, *Diplomacy,* New York: Simon and Schuster, 1994.

Krasner, Stephen, 'Approaches to the state: Alternative conceptions and historical dynamics', *Comparative Politics,* 1984, vol. 16, pp. 223–46.

——, *Sovereignty: Organized Hypocrisy,* Princeton, NJ: Princeton University Press, 1999.

Krasner, Stephen D., 'Are bureaucracies important? (or Allison Wonderland)' *Foreign Policy,* 1972, no. 7, pp. 159–79.

Kuhn, Thomas S., *The Structure of Scientific Revolutions,* Chicago, IL: University of Chicago Press, 1962.

Lawson, George, 'A conversation with Michael Mann', *Millennium,* 2005, vol. 34, no. 2, pp. 477–85.

Lawson, George, 'The promise of historical sociology in international relations', *International Studies Review,* 2006, vol. 8, no. 3, pp. 397–423.

Lawson, George, John M. Hobson, Linda Weiss, Fred Halliday and Michael Mann, 'The work of Michael Mann', *Millennium,* 2005, vol. 34, no. 2, pp. 476–552.

Leander, Anna, '"Globalisation theory": Feeble … and hijacked', *International Political Sociology,* 2009, vol. 3, pp. 109–12.

Lebow, Richard Ned, 'The Cuban missile crisis: Reading the lessons correctly', *Political Studies Quarterly,* vol. 98, no. 3, 1983, pp. 431–58.

Lee, Donna and James Hamill , 'A middle power paradox? South African diplomacy in the post-apartheid era', *International Relations,* 2001, vol. 15, no. 4, pp. 33–59.

Lehman, Howard P. and Jennifer L. Mckoy, 'The dynamics of the two-level bargaining game: The 1988 Brazilian debt negotiations', *World Politics,* 1992, vol. 44, no. 2, pp. 600–44.

Leifer, Michael, *Dictionary of the Modern Politics of Southeast Asia,* Oxford: Routledge, 1995.

Levy, Gilat and Ronny Razin, 'It takes two: An explanation for the democratic peace', *Journal of the European Economic Association*, 2004, vol. 2, no. 2, pp. 1–29.

Levy, Jack, 'Learning and foreign policy: Sweeping a conceptual minefield', *International Organization*, 1994, vol. 48, no. 2, pp. 279–312.

Light, Margot, 'Foreign policy analysis', in A.J.R. Groom and Margot Light (eds), *Contemporary International Relations: A Guide to Theory*, London: Pinter, 1994, pp. 93–108.

Lindblom, Charles E., 'The science of muddling through', *Public Administration Review*, 1959, vol. 19, no. 2, pp. 79–88.

Linz, Juan, 'Transitions to democracy' *Washington Quarterly*, 1990, vol. 13, no. 3, pp. 133–42.

Linz, Juan and Alfred Stepen, *Problems of Transition and Consolidation*, Baltimore, MD: Johns Hopkins University Press, 1996.

Lipson, Michael, 'Between Iraq and a hard place: UN arms inspections and the politics of Security Council Resolution 1441', paper presented at Midwest Political Science Association, 20 April, 2006.

McGrew, Anthony, 'Globalization and Global Politics' in John Baylis and Steve Smith (eds) *The Globalization of World Politics*, Oxford: Oxford University Press, 2005.

Maher, Imelda, Stijn Billiet and Dermot Hodson, 'The principal-agent approach to EU studies: Apply liberally but handle with care', *Comparative European Politics*, 2009, vol. 7, no. 4, pp. 409–13

Mann, Michael, *The Sources of Social Power: The Rise of Classes and Nation-States, 1760–1914*, Cambridge: Cambridge University Press, 1993.

——, 'As the twentieth century ages', *New Left Review*, 1995, vol. 21, no. 4, pp. 104–24.

——, 'Has globalization ended the rise and rise of the nation-state?', *Review of International Political Economy*, 1997, vol. 4, no. 3, pp. 472–96.

——, 'Globalization and September 11', *New Left Review*, 2001, vol. 12, no. 4, pp. 51–72.

Mansbach, Richard, Yale Ferguson and Donald Lampert, *The Web of World Politics: Nonstate Actors in the Global System*, Englewood Cliffs; NJ: Prentice Hall, 1976.

Mansfield, Edward and Jack Snyder, 'Democratisation and war', *Foreign Affairs*, 1995, May/June, pp. 79–97.

Mansfield, Edward and Jack Snyder, *Electing to Fight: Why Emerging Democracies Go To War*, Cambridge, MA: MIT Press, 2005.

Marais, Hein, *South Africa: The Limits to Change*, London: Zed, 2001.

Marx, Karl, *The Communist Manifesto*, London: Penguin, 1967.

Mehler, Andreas, 'Eternal plight: France in search of a new Africa policy', *Spiegel Online International*, 4 November 2008, www.spiegal.de/international/world/0c1518,546796,00.html, accessed 5 April 2011.

Mersheimer, John and Walt M. Stephen, *The Israel Lobby*, London: Penguin, 2007.

Mills, Charles Wright, *The Power Elite*, Oxford: Oxford University Press, 1956.

Milner, Helen, *Interests, Institutions and Information: Domestic Politics and International Relations*, Princeton, NJ: Princeton University Press, 1997.

Mintz, Alex (ed.), *Integrating Cognitive and Rational Theories of Foreign Policy: The Poliheuristic Theory of Decision*, Cambridge: Cambridge University Press, 2004.

Moon, Bruce, 'The state in foreign and domestic policy', in Laura Neack, Jeanne Hey and Patrick Haney (eds), *Foreign Policy Analysis: Continuity and Change in its Second Generation*, Englewood Cliffs, NJ: Prentice Hall, 1995, pp. 192–9.

Morgenthau, Hans, *Politics Among Nations*, New York: Knopf, 1948.

Morse, Edward L., 'Modernization and the transformation of foreign policies: Modernization, interdependence and externalization', *World Politics,* 1970, vol. 22, no. 3, pp. 371–92.

Muller, Haral and Thomas Risse-Kappen, 'From the outside in and from the inside out', in David Skidmore and Valerie M. Hudson, *The Limits of State Autonomy*, Boulder, CO: Westview Press, 1993.

Neack, Laura, 'Linking state type with foreign policy behaviour' in Laura Neack, Jeanne Hey and Patrick Haney (eds) *Foreign Policy Analysis: Continuity and Change in its Second Generation*, Englewood Cliffs, NJ: Prentice Hall, 1995.

Neack, Laura, Jeanne Hey and Patrick Haney (eds), *Foreign Policy Analysis: Continuity and Change in its Second Generation,* Englewood Cliffs, NJ: Prentice Hall, 1995.

Neustadt, Richard E., *Presidential Power: The Politics of Leadership*, New York: Wiley, 1960.

Ninic, Miroslav, *Democracy and Foreign Policy: The Fallacy of Political Realism*, New York: Columbia University Press, 1992.

Nye, Joseph S., *Soft Power: The Means to Success in World Politics*, New York: Public Affairs, 2006.

Nye, Joseph S. and Robert O. Keohane (eds), *Transnational Relations and World Politics* Cambridge, MA: Harvard University Press, 1970.

Nye, Joseph S. and Robert O. Keohane, 'Globalization: What's new? What's not? (And so what?)', *Foreign Policy,* 2000, vol. 118, no. 1, pp. 104–20.

Orbovich, Cynthia and Richard Molnar, 'Modeling foreign policy advisory processes', in Eric Singer and Valerie Hudson (eds) *Political Psychology and Foreign Policy*, Boulder, CO: Westview, 1992.

Ougaard, Morten and Richard Higgott, *Towards Global Polity: Future Trends and Prospects*, London: Routledge, 2002.

Owen, Roger, *State, Power and Politics in the Making of the Modern Middle East*, London: Routledge, 2004.

Payne, Richard J. and Eddie Ganaway, 'The influence of black Americans on US policy towards Southern Africa', *African Affairs*, 1980, vol. 79, pp. 567–85.

Peri, Yoram, *Generals in the Cabinet Room: How the Military Shapes Israeli Policy*, Washington, DC: The United States Institute for Peace, 2006.

Peters, B. Guy, *Institutional Theory in Political Science: The 'New Institutionalism'*, 2nd edn, London: Continuum, 2005.

Pinto-Duchinsky, Michael, 'Foreign political aid: The German party foundations and their US counterparts', *International Affairs*, 1991, vol. 67, no. 1, pp. 33–63.

Powell, Robert, *Nuclear Deterrence Theory*, New York: Cambridge University Press, 1990.

Putnam, Robert, 'Diplomacy and domestic politics: The logic of two-level games', *International Organization*, 1988, vol. 42, no. 3, pp. 427–60.

Randolf, Rummel, 'Democracies are less warlike than other regimes', *European Journal of International Relations*, 1995, vol. 1, no. 4, pp. 649–64.

Renshon, Jonathan and Stanley Renshon, 'Theory and practice of foreign policy decision making', *Political Psychology*, 2008, vol. 29, no. 4, pp. 509–36.

Ripley, Brian, 'Cognition, culture and bureaucratic politics' in Laura Neack, Jeanne Hey and Patrick Haney (eds), *Foreign Policy Analysis: Continuity and Change in its Second Generation*, Englewood Cliffs, NJ: Prentice Hall, 1995.

Risse-Kappen, Thomas, 'Public opinion, domestic structure and foreign policy in liberal democracies', *World Politics*, 1991, vol. 43, pp. 491–517.

——(ed.), *Bringing Transnational Relations Back In: Non-State Actors, Domestic Structures, and International Institutions*, Cambridge: Cambridge University Press, 1995.

——, 'Democratic peace – warlike democracies? A social constructivist interpretation of the liberal argument', *European Journal of International Relations*, 1995, vol. 1, no. 4, pp. 491–517.

Robertson, Roland, 'Differentiational reductionism and the missing link in Albert's approach to globalisation theory', *International Political Sociology*, 2009, vol. 3, pp. 119–22.

Robinson, Piers, 'Theorizing the influence of media on world politics', *European Journal of Communication*, 2001, vol. 16, no. 4, pp. 523–44.

Rochester, Martin, 'The paradigm debate in international relations and its implications for foreign policy making: Toward a redefinition of the "national interest"', *Western Political Quarterly*, 1978, vol. 31, no. 1, pp. 48–58.

Rosati, Jerel A., 'Developing a systemic decision-making framework: Bureaucratic politics in perspective', *World Politics*, 1981, vol. 33, no. 2, pp. 234–52.

——, 'A cognitive guide to the study of foreign policy', in Laura Neack, Jeanne Hey and Patrick Haney (eds), *Foreign Policy Analysis: Continuity and Change in its Second Generation*, Englewood Cliffs, NJ: Prentice Hall, 1995.

Rosati, Jerel A., Joe Hagan and Martin Sampson (eds), *Foreign Policy Restructuring*, Columbia: University of South Carolina, 1994.

Rosenau, James, *Public Opinion and Foreign Policy*, New York: Random House, 1961.

——, 'Pre-theories and theories and foreign policy', in R.B. Farrell (ed.), *Approaches to Comparative and International Politics*, Evanston, IL: Northwestern University Press, 1966.

——, (ed.), *Domestic Sources of Foreign Policy*, New York: Free Press, 1967.

——, 'A pre-theory revisited: World politics in an era of cascading inter-dependence', *International Studies Quarterly*, 1984, vol. 28, no. 3, pp. 245–305.

——, *Along the Domestic–Foreign Frontier: Exploring Governance in a Turbulent World*, Cambridge: Cambridge University Press, 1997.

Rosenberg, Justin, 'Globalisation theory: A post mortem', *International Politics*, 2005, vol. 42, no. 1, pp. 2–74.

Rummel, Randolf, *National Attributes and Behavior*, Beverley Hills, CA: Sage, 1979.

——, 'Democracies are less warlike than other regimes', *European Journal of International Relations*, 1995, vol. 1, no. 4, pp. 649–64.

Russet, Bruce M., *Grasping the Democratic Peace: Principles for a Post-Cold War World*, Princeton, NJ: Princeton University Press, 1993.

Salmore, Barbara and Stephen Salmore, 'Political regimes and foreign policy', in Maurice East, Stephen Salmore and Charles Hermann (eds), *Why Nations Act: Theoretical Perspectives for Comparative Foreign Policy*, Beverly Hills, CA: Sage, 1978.

Schelling, Thomas, *The Strategy of Conflict*, Cambridge, MA: Harvard University Press, 1960.

Schilling, Roller W., Paul Y. Hammond and Glenn H. Snyder, *Strategy, Politics, and Defense Budgets*, New York: Columbia University, Institute of War and Peace Studies, 1962.

Scholte, Jan Aart, 'Premature obituaries: A response to Justin Rosenberg', *International Politics*, 2005, vol. 42, no. 3, pp. 390–9.

——, *Globalization: A Critical Introduction*, Basingstoke: Palgrave Macmillan, 2005.

Scholte, Jan Aart and Ronald Robertson, *Encyclopedia of Globalisation*, New York: Routledge, 2007.

Scott Thomas, *The Diplomacy of Liberation: The Foreign Relations of the ANC since 1960*, London: Tauris Academic, 1995.

Shapiro, Robert Y. and Robert I. Page, 'Foreign policy and the rational public', *Journal of Conflict Resolution*, 1988, vol. 32, no. 2, pp. 211–47.

Shaw, Martin, 'The state of globalization: Towards a theory of state transformation' *Review of International Political Economy,* 1997, vol. 4, no. 3, pp. 497–513.

——, 'The historical sociology of the future', *Review of International Political Economy*, 1998, vol. 5, no. 2, pp. 321–6.

——, *Theory of the Global State: Globalization as an Unfinished Revolution*, Cambridge: Cambridge University Press, 2001.

Shepard, Graham, 'Personality effects on American foreign policy, 1969–84: A second test of interpersonal generalization theory', *International Studies Quarterly*, 1988, vol. 32, no. 1, pp. 91–123.

Shy, John 'The American military experience: History and learning', *Journal of Interdisciplinary History*, 1971, vol. 1, no. 2, pp. 205–28.

Sigal, Leon, 'The rational policy model and the Formosa Straits crisis', *International Studies Quarterly*, 1970, vol. 14, no. 2, 121–56.

Singer, J. David, 'The level-of-analysis problem in international relations', *World Politics*, 1961, vol. 14, no. 1, pp. 77–92.

Skidmore, David, 'The politics of national security policy: Interest groups, coalitions and the SALT II debate', in David Skidmore and Valerie Hudson (eds), *The Limits of State Autonomy: Society Groups and Foreign Policy Formulation*, Boulder, CO: Westview, 1993.

Skidmore, David and Valerie Hudson (eds), *The Limits of State Autonomy: Society Groups and Foreign Policy Formulation*, Boulder, CO: Westview, 1993.

Skocpol, Theda, *States and Social Revolutions: A Comparative Analysis of France, Russia, and China*, Cambridge: Cambridge University Press, 1979.

Smith, Karen, *European Union Foreign Policy in a Changing World*, Cambridge: Polity, 2008.

Smith, Steve, 'Allison and the Cuban missile crisis: A review of the bureaucratic politics model of foreign policy decision-making', *Millennium*, 1980, vol. 9, no. 1, pp. 21–40.

Smith, Steve, Amelia Hadfield and Tim Dunne, *Foreign Policy: Theories, Actors, Cases*, Oxford: Oxford University Press, 2008.

Snyder, Gary and Paul Diesing, *Conflict Among Nations: Bargaining, Decision Making and System Structure in International Crises*, Princeton, NJ: Princeton University Press, 1977.

Snyder, Richard, Henry W. Bruck and Burton Sapin, *Foreign Policy Decision-Making: An Approach to the Study of International Politics*, New York: Free Press/Macmillan, 1962.

Snyder, Richard, Henry W. Bruck and Burton Sapin, 'Decision making as an approach to the study of international politics', in Richard Snyder, Henry W. Bruck and Burton Sapin (eds), *Foreign Policy Decision-Making: An Approach to the Study of International Politics*, New York: Free Press/ Macmillan, 1962.

Sorenson, George, 'Sovereignty: Change and continuity in a fundamental institution', *Political Studies*, 1999, vol. 47, pp. 590–604.

Sprout, Harold and Margaret Sprout, *Man–Milieu Relationship Hypotheses in the Context of International Politics*, Princeton, NJ: Princeton University Press, 1956.

Spruyt, Hendrik, 'Historical sociology and systems theory in international relations', *Review of International Political Economy*, 1998, vol. 5, no. 2, pp. 340–53.

Stanger, Alison, 'Democratization and the international system', in Miles Kahler (ed.), *Liberalization and Foreign Policy*, New York: Columbia University Press, 1997.

Stein, Janice S., 'Political learning by doing: Gorbachev as uncommitted thinker and motivated learner', *International Organization*, 1994, vol. 48, no. 2, pp. 155–83.

Steinbruner, John, *The Cybernetic Theory of Decision*, Princeton, NJ: Princeton University Press, 1974.

Steiner, Miriam, 'The elusive essence of decision: A critical comparison of Allison's and Snyder's decision-making approaches', *International Studies Quarterly*, 1977, vol. 21, no. 2, pp. 389–422.

Stone, Diane, 'Think tanks – beyond nation states', in Diane Stone and Andrew Denham (eds), *Think Tank Traditions: Policy Research and the Politics of Ideas,* Manchester: Manchester University Press, 2004.

't Hart, Paul and Uriel Roenthal, 'Reappraising bureaucratic politics', *Mershon International Studies Review*, 1998, vol. 42, no. 2, pp. 236–7.

't Hart, Paul, Eric Stern and and Bengt Sundelius, *Beyond Groupthink: Political Group Dynamics and Foreign Policy-making*, Ann Arbor: University of Michigan Press, 1997.

Tarar, Ahmer, 'International bargaining with two-sided domestic constraints', *Journal of Conflict Resolution*, 2001, vol. 45, no. 3, pp. 320–40.

Tsebelis, George, *Nested Games: Rational Choice in Comparative Politics*, Berkeley: University of California Press, 1990.

Vertzberger, Yaacov, 'Foreign policy decision-makers as practical intuitive historians: Applied history and its shortcomings', *International Studies Quarterly*, 1986, vol. 30, no. 2, pp. 223–47.

de Waal, Alex, *Famine Crimes: Politics and the Disaster Relief Industry in Africa*, Bloomington: Indiana University Press, 1997.

Wallace, William and Daphne Josselin (eds), *Non-State Actors in World Politics*, London: Palgrave, 2002.

Waltz, Kenneth, 'International politics is not foreign policy', *Security Studies,* 1996, vol. 6, no. 1, pp. 54–7.

Webber, Mark and Michael Smith (eds), *Foreign Policy in a Transformed World*, Harlow: Prentice Hall, 2002.

Welch, David A., 'The organizational process and bureaucratic politics paradigms: retrospect and prospect', *International Security'*, 1992, vol. 17, no. 2, pp. 119–146.

Welch, David, *Painful Choices: A Theory of Foreign Policy Change*, Princeton, NJ: Princeton Uuniversity Press, 2005.

Weldes, Jutta, 'Bureaucratic politics: A critical constructivist assessment', *Mershon International Studies Review*, 1998, vol. 42, no. 2, pp. 216–225.

——, *Constructing National Interests: The United States and the Cuban Missile Crisis*, Minneapolis: University of Minnesota Press, 1999.

White, Brian, 'Analysing foreign policy problems and approaches', in Michael Clarke and Brian White (eds), *Understanding Foreign Policy*, Cheltenham: Edward Elgar, 1989.

Winter, David G., 'Personality and foreign policy: Historical overview of research', in Eric Singer and Valerie Hudson (eds), *Political Psychology and Foreign Policy*, Boulder, CO: Westview, 1992.

Wright, Stephen (ed.), *African Foreign Policies*, Boulder, CO: Westview, 1999.

Wurfel, David and Bruce Burton (eds), *The Political Economy of Foreign Policy in Southeast Asia*, Basingstoke: Macmillan, 1990.

Index